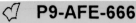
THE POCKET
THICH NHAT HANH

THE POCKET
THICH NHAT HANH

Compiled and Edited by
MELVIN McLEOD

SHAMBHALA
Boulder
2012

Shambhala Publications, Inc.
4720 Walnut Street
Boulder, Colorado 80301
www.shambhala.com

© 2012 by the Unified Buddhist Church

13 12 11 10 9 8

Printed in Canada

♾ This edition is printed on acid-free paper that meets the
American National Standards Institute z39.48 Standard.
♻ This book is printed on 100% postconsumer recycled paper.
For more information please visit www.shambhala.com.
Distributed in the United States by Penguin Random House
LLC and in Canada by Random House of Canada Ltd

See page 229 for Library of Congress
Cataloging-in-Publication data.

CONTENTS

Editor's Introduction   xi

1. MINDFULNESS   1

A Life of Miracles   3

Your True Home   6

Concentration   9

Freedom   12

Resting   14

Loving Presence   19

Mindfulness of Breath   21

Walk Like a Buddha   26

Touching the Earth   30

Mindful Living   32

Ruling the Five Skandhas   35

CONTENTS

Habit Energy 40

Darkness Becomes Light 43

A Day of Mindfulness 46

2. ENLIGHTENMENT 53

Interbeing 55

The Buddha 58

Impermanence 62

Deep Seeing 66

Nothing to Attain 70

Beyond Birth and Death 73

Pure Land 77

The Two Dimensions 81

Hide and Seek 85

No Fear 87

The Zen Master 89

Three Doors of Liberation 92

The Businessless Person 96

CONTENTS

Smile of the Bodhisattva 100

Right Path 104

3. EMOTIONS AND RELATIONSHIPS 109

The Wounded Child Inside 111

Appropriate Attention 115

The Second Arrow 117

Seeds 119

Blocks and Knots 123

Weathering Strong Emotions 126

Taking Care of Your Anger 128

Mindfulness of Consumption 131

Hugging Meditation 134

The Energy of Love 137

Understanding 139

Four Mantras 141

Mindful Communication 147

Your True Person 151

CONTENTS

Wrong Perceptions   153

Letting Go   157

Inferiority   159

Healing the Past   162

Walking with Your Parents   165

4. PEACE   171

The Spiritual Dimension
of Politics   173

Seeds of Violence   175

Engaged Buddhism   178

Heroism   181

The Thousand Arms
of the Bodhisattva   183

The Peaceful Revolution   187

Labels   190

Inclusiveness   192

Reconciliation   196

CONTENTS

Children of the Earth 198

Art 202

Peace Work 205

The Five Mindfulness Trainings 208

Sources 217
Credits 223

EDITOR'S INTRODUCTION

WE GAUGE THE GREATNESS of spiritual teachers by the depth, breadth, and impact of their teachings, and by the example their lives set for us. By all these measures, Thich Nhat Hanh is one of the leading spiritual masters of our age. In fact, when the time has come to judge such things, I think he will be considered one of history's great Buddhist masters.

Like a mighty river, the teachings of Thich Nhat Hanh are deep and wide. What can be said of their depth, indeed the deepness of any spiritual teaching? Profundity must be experienced; it cannot be described. These teachings cannot be fathomed by words. All I can say is that you should not be misled by their apparent simplicity, by their directness, practicality, and relevance that could be taken for a lack of philosophical sophistication. It takes a long and hard journey to arrive at such clarity, in which the problems of life are finally resolved in plain, essential language that makes deep truths available to all who want to see them. Far more than the opposite, such purity and simplicity of language is the hallmark of true profundity.

I have tried in this book to select excerpts from Thich Nhat Hanh's large body of published work that honor the depth of his teachings, choosing passages that I feel epitomize most effectively his key insights and instructions. Yet as your experience of these teachings will be personal and subjective, so is mine. As a student of Buddhism for many years, all I could do—and can the editor of such a book ever do anything else?—is to select those passages that touch my own heart, life, and practice most deeply. All I can hope is that they touch you too.

Just as challenging is to reflect the unique breadth of this great master's teachings. No other Buddhist teacher today—perhaps no spiritual teacher in any tradition—addresses such a wide range of important questions, from the personal to the global.

Thich Nhat Hanh has written more than seventy books and given innumerable hours of personal teachings over a career of more than sixty years. His writings range from in-depth dissertations on Buddhist philosophy and popular works on Buddhist practice to political works, psychology, poetry, history, children's books, and fiction.

In surveying this vast body of writings, my aspiration is that this book will introduce you to the themes in Thich Nhat Hanh's work that are most important for the Buddhist practitioner and general reader. Organizing these diverse teachings is necessarily a subjective exercise. In my own study and practice of his teachings, I have found that they fall into four broad categories: Mindfulness, Enlightenment, Emotions and Relationships, and Peace.

The opening section of this anthology, Mindfulness, includes many of the teachings for which Thich Nhat Hanh is most famous. Like all great Buddhist masters, he is above all a teacher of meditation. He offers us profound and practical methods we can use both in our formal meditation practice and in our lives. Whether they are in plain or poetic language, these teachings strike right at the heart of life. If we can truly follow his instructions, even for a moment, they will transform us on the spot, filling our lives with joy, enjoyment, and virtue.

From that place, our true home, as

Thich Nhat Hanh calls it, he takes us on an even more transformative journey, into the most profound truths of Buddhism. So in the second section of this book, Enlightenment, we learn about a path that takes us beyond ignorance, beyond struggle, beyond birth and death itself. This is the journey to complete liberation, and it can start right now. In this section we see Thich Nhat Hanh not just as a teacher of popular spirituality but as a deeply realized Buddhist teacher, speaking to us directly from his experience of true liberation. Like all great Buddhist masters, he speaks to us with the voice of the Buddha.

In section three, Emotions and Relationships, we return to our daily lives in this modern world—the ups and downs, the joys and sorrows, the suffering we cause others and the pain they cause us. I don't know how this elderly Vietnamese monk understands us so well, but he offers some of the most helpful and practical advice anywhere for working with our psychological wounds and relationship problems. Beginning with the traditional Buddhist understanding of the workings of mind, he shows us a powerful path to healing our wounded modern psyches. Since it is the wounds within us that beget the wounds we inflict on others, this is also the path to healthy and loving relationships. It is, finally, the path to a healthy and loving world.

In the Mahayana Buddhist tradition from which Thich Nhat Hanh comes, personal liberation is never enough. Until all are healed, none is healed. This is the way a bodhisattva like Thich Nhat Hanh sees the world. He is renowned as the founder of the Engaged Buddhist movement, and in the final section of this book, Peace, we sample his teachings on politics, society, and the environment. All these teachings, ultimately, are about creating peace—between people, between religions, between nations, between humanity and the earth. And since peace always begins within us, this book concludes with Thich Nhat Hanh's famed Five Mindfulness Trainings, a discipline of peace, ethics, and caring to transform our lives, our relationships, and our society.

Thich Nhat Hanh's life story is itself an inspiration. This is a man who has put his life on the line for peace, who has given his all for the benefit of others. As a young monk in his native Vietnam, he was a vigorous reformer of traditional Buddhism who went on to become a leader of the Vietnamese peace movement. It was then, at great personal risk, that he laid down the principles of Engaged Buddhism that continue to inspire us today. His impartial campaign against violence earned him the enmity of hard-liners on both sides, and when he traveled to the West in 1966 to campaign for peace, the government of South Vietnam would not let him return home.

That lone Buddhist monk, exiled and without resources, has since touched the lives of countless people. Tens of thousands around the world consider him their personal teacher; his writings have inspired millions more and helped shape Buddhism as we know it today. His impact is profound. Like so many, I have benefited from the life and teachings of Thich Nhat Hanh. May they benefit your life too.

Melvin McLeod
Editor-in-chief
The Shambhala Sun
Buddhadharma: The Practitioner's Quarterly

I

MINDFULNESS

A LIFE OF MIRACLES

As we sit down next to a stream, we can listen to its laughter and watch its sparkling waters, noticing the pebbles glistening and the fresh green plants nearby, and we may be overcome with happiness. We are one with the stream's freshness, purity, and clarity. But in just an instant we may find we've had enough. Our heart is troubled, and we think of other things. We are no longer at one with the stream.

It is of no use to sit in a peaceful forest if our mind is lost in the city. When we live with a child or a friend, their freshness and warmth can relax us. But if our heart is not with them, their precious presence is neglected, and they no longer exist. We must be aware of them to appreciate their value, to allow them to be our happiness. If through carelessness and forgetfulness we become dissatisfied with them, and begin asking too much of them or reprimanding them, we will lose them. Only after they are gone will we realize their preciousness and feel regret. But once they are gone, all our regrets are in vain.

Around us, life bursts forth with miracles—a glass of water, a ray of sunshine, a leaf, a caterpillar, a flower, laughter, raindrops. If you live in awareness, it is easy to see miracles everywhere. Each human being is a multiplicity of miracles. Eyes that see thousands of colors, shapes, and forms; ears that hear a bee flying or a thunderclap; a brain that ponders a speck of dust as easily as the entire cosmos; a heart that beats in rhythm with the heartbeat of all beings. When we are tired and feel discouraged by life's daily struggles, we may not notice these miracles, but they are always there.

Have a look at the apple tree in your yard. Look at it with complete attention. It is truly a miracle. If you notice it, you will take good care of it, and you too are part of its miraculousness. Even after you have cared for it for only a week, its leaves are already greener and shinier. It is exactly the same with the people who are around you. Under the influence of awareness, you become more attentive, understanding, and loving, and your presence not only nourishes you and makes you lovelier, it enhances them as well. Our entire society can be changed by one person's peaceful presence.

Our minds create everything. The majestic mountaintop, brilliant with snow, is you yourself when you contemplate it. Its existence depends on your awareness. When you close your eyes, as long as your mind is present, the mountain is there. Sitting in meditation, with several sense-windows closed, you feel the presence of the whole universe. Why? Because the mind is there. If your eyes are closed, it is so that you can see better. The sights and sounds of the world are not your enemies. Your enemy is forgetfulness, the absence of mindfulness.

YOUR TRUE HOME

Your true home is in the here and the now. It is not limited by time, space, nationality, or race. Your true home is not an abstract idea; it is something you can touch and live in every moment. With mindfulness and concentration, the energies of the Buddha, you can find your true home in the full relaxation of your mind and body in the present moment. No one can take it away from you. Other people can occupy your country, they can even put you in prison, but they cannot take away your true home and your freedom.

When we stop speaking and thinking and enjoy deeply our in- and out-breath, we are enjoying being in our true home and we can touch deeply the wonders of life. This is the path shown to us by the Buddha. When you breathe in, you bring all yourself together, body and mind; you become one. Equipped with that energy of mindfulness and concentration, you may take a step. And if you can take one mindful step, you can take another and another. You have the insight that this is your true home—you are alive, you are fully present, you are touching life as a reality. Your true home is a solid reality that you can touch with your feet, with your hands, and with your mind.

It is fundamental that you touch your true home and realize your true home in the here and the now. All of us have the seed of mindfulness and concentration in us. By taking a mindful breath or a mindful step, you can bring your mind back to your body. In your daily life, your body and mind often go in two different directions. You are in a state of distraction, mind in one place, body in another. Your body is putting on a coat but your mind is preoccupied, caught in the past or the future. But between your mind and your body there is something: your breath. As soon as you go home to your breath and you breathe with awareness, your body and mind come together very quickly. While breathing in, you don't think of anything; you just focus your attention on your in-breath. You focus; you invest 100 percent of yourself in your in-breath. You become your in-breath. There is a concentration on your in-breath that will make body and mind come together in just one moment. And suddenly you find yourself fully present, fully alive.

CONCENTRATION

Joy and happiness are born of concentration. When you are having a cup of tea, the value of that experience depends on your concentration. You have to drink the tea with 100 percent of your being. The true pleasure is experienced in the concentration. When you walk and you are 100 percent concentrated, the joy you get from the steps you are taking is much greater than the joy you would get without concentration. You have to invest 100 percent of your body and mind in the act of walking. Then you will experience that being alive and taking steps on this planet are miraculous things.

The Zen master Linji (also known as

Rinzai) said, "The miracle is walking on the earth, not walking on water or fire. The real miracle is walking on this earth." Why should you not perform a miracle just by walking? A step taken with mindfulness can lead you to the Kingdom of God. This is possible. You can do it today. Life is too precious for us to lose ourselves in our ideas and concepts, in our anger and our despair. We must wake up to the marvelous reality of life. We must begin to live fully and truly, every moment of our daily lives.

When you are holding a cup of tea in your hand, do it while being 100 percent there. You know how to do this—one deep in-breath, one gentle out-breath, and the body and mind come together. You are truly there, absolutely alive, fully present! This only takes ten or fifteen seconds, and suddenly the tea reveals itself to you in all its splendor and wonder.

When I pick up a book or open a door, I

want to invest myself in this act 100 percent. This is what I learned during my monastic training, when my teacher taught me how to offer a stick of incense. A stick of incense is very small and very light, yet the right way to hold it is with two hands. When offering the incense, you have to invest 100 percent of your being in your hands and in two of your fingers—the energy of mindfulness must be concentrated there. This may look like a ritual, but it is really an act of concentrated awareness. I put my left hand on my right hand, and during this time, I concentrate 100 percent. The incense is an offering to the Buddha, but does the Buddha really need incense? This is actually an offering of peace, of joy, and of concentration.

FREEDOM

The basic condition of happiness is freedom. If there is something on your mind that you keep thinking about, then you are caught and have no freedom. If you are caught in sorrow and regret about the past, or if you are anxious about what will happen to you in the future, then you are not really free to enjoy the many wonders of life that are available in the here and now. The blue sky, the beautiful trees, the lovely faces of children, the flowers, and the birds can nourish and heal us in the present moment.

Many people in our society are not happy, even though the conditions for their happiness already exist. Their "habit energy" is always pushing them ahead, preventing them from being happy in the here and now. But with a little bit of training, we can all learn to recognize this energy every time it comes up. Why wait to be happy? When you walk, it is possible to walk in such a way that every step becomes nourishing and healing. This is not difficult.

Whether you are a businessperson walking across the office, a congressperson walking up the Capitol steps, or a police officer out on the streets, it is always possible to practice mindful walking and to enjoy every step you take. If you know the art of mindful walking, then you will be fully present in the here and now. You make yourself available to life and life becomes available to you.

Every one of us has the tendency to run. We have run all of our lives, and we continue to run into the future where we think that some happiness may be waiting. We have received the habit of running from our parents and ancestors. When we learn to recognize our habit of running, we can use mindful breathing, and simply smile at this habit and say, "Hello, my dear old friend, I know you are there." And then you are free from this habit energy. You don't have to fight it. There is no fighting in this practice. There is only recognition and awareness of what is going on. When the habit energy of running manifests itself, you just smile and come back to your mindful breathing. Then you are free from it, and you continue to breathe in, breathe out, and enjoy the present moment.

RESTING

My dear friends, suppose someone is holding a pebble and throws it in the air and the pebble begins to fall down into a river. After the pebble touches the surface of the water, it allows itself to sink slowly into the river. It will reach the bed of the river without any effort. Once the pebble is at the bottom of the river, it continues to rest. It allows the water to pass by.

I think the pebble reaches the bed of the river by the shortest path because it allows itself to fall without making any effort. During our sitting meditation we can allow ourselves to rest like a pebble. We can allow ourselves to sink naturally without effort to the position of sitting, the position of resting. Resting is a very important practice; we have to learn the art of resting.

Resting is the first part of Buddhist meditation. You should allow your body and your mind to rest. Our mind as well as our body needs to rest. The problem is that not many of us know how to allow our body and mind to rest. We are always struggling; struggling has become a kind of habit. We cannot resist being active, struggling all the time. We struggle even during our sleep. It is very important to realize that we have the habit energy of struggling. We have to be able to recognize a habit when it manifests itself because if we know how to recognize our habit, it will lose its energy and will not be able to push us anymore.

To meditate means first of all to be there—to be on your cushion, to be on your walking meditation path. Eating also is a meditation if you are really there, present 100 percent with your food. The essential is to be there. So please when you practice meditation, don't make any effort. Allow yourself to be like that pebble at rest. The pebble is resting at the bottom of the river and the pebble does not have to do anything. While you are walking, you are resting. While you are sitting, you are resting.

If you struggle during your sitting meditation or walking meditation, you are not doing it right. The Buddha said, "My practice is the practice of non-practice." That means a lot. Give up all struggle. Allow yourself to be, to rest.

When I sit on my meditation cushion, I consider it to be something very pleasant. I don't struggle at all on my cushion. I allow myself to be, to rest. I don't make any effort and that is why I do not get any trouble while sitting. While sitting I do not struggle and that is why all my muscles are relaxed. If you struggle during your sitting meditation, you will very soon have pain in your shoulders and back. But if you allow yourself to be rested on your cushion you can sit for a very long time, and each minute is light, refreshing, nourishing, and healing.

We do not sit in order to struggle to get enlightenment. No. Sitting first of all is for the pleasure of sitting. Walking first of all is for the pleasure of walking. And eating is for the pleasure of eating. And the art is to be there 100 percent.

Be there truly. Be there 100 percent of yourself. In every moment of your daily life. That is the essence of true Buddhist meditation. Each of us knows that we can do that, so let us train to live each moment of our daily life deeply. That is why I like to define mindfulness as the energy that helps us to be there 100 percent. It is the energy of your true presence.

Breathing in, repeat *in the here, in the here*. Breathing out—*in the now, in the now*. Although these are different words they mean exactly the same thing. I have arrived in the here. I have arrived in the now. I am home in the here. I am home in the now.

When you practice like that, you practice stopping. Stopping is the basic Buddhist practice of meditation. You stop running. You stop struggling. You allow yourself to rest, to heal, to calm.

LOVING PRESENCE

The miracle of mindfulness is, first of all, that you are here. Being truly here is very important—being here for yourself, and for the one you love. How can you love if you are not here? A fundamental condition for love is your own presence. In order to love, you must be here. That is certain. Fortunately, being here is not a difficult thing to accomplish. It is enough to breathe and let go of thinking or planning. Just come back to yourself, concentrate on your breath, and smile. You are here, body and mind together. You are here, alive, completely alive. That is a miracle.

Some people live as though they are already dead. There are people moving around us who are consumed by their past, terrified of their future, and stuck in their anger and jealousy. They are not alive; they are just walking corpses. If you look around yourself with mindfulness, you will see people going around like zombies. Have a great deal of compassion for the people around you who are living like this. They do not know that life is accessible only in the here and now.

We must practice resurrection, and this is an everyday practice. With an in-breath, you bring your mind back to your body. In this way you become alive in the here and now. Joy, peace, and happiness are possible. You have an appointment with life, an appointment that is in the here and now.

It is necessary to come back to the present moment in order to touch life in a deep way. We all have the ability to walk in the Kingdom of God, to walk in the Pure Land of Buddha every day. You have all you need—legs, lungs, eyes, and mind—and with a little bit of practice, you can generate the energy of mindfulness within you, just like lighting a lamp. Once you have become truly alive, take a step and you will enter the Pure Land. You will enter into the Kingdom of God.

The Kingdom of God is not a mere notion. It is a reality that can be touched in everyday life. The Kingdom of God is now or never, and we all have the ability to touch it—not only with our minds, but with our feet. The energy of mindfulness helps you in this. With one mindful step, you touch the Kingdom of God.

MINDFULNESS OF BREATH

The way to maintain your presence in the here and now is through mindfulness of the breath. There is no need to manipulate the breath. Breath is a natural thing, like air, like light; we should leave it as it is and not interfere with it. What we are doing is simply lighting up the lamp of awareness to illuminate our breathing. We generate the energy of mindfulness to illuminate everything that is happening in the present moment.

As you breathe in, you can say to yourself, "Breathing in, I know that I am breathing in." When you do this, the energy of mindfulness embraces your in-breath, just like sunlight touching the leaves and branches of a tree. The light of mindfulness is content just to be there and embrace the breath, without doing it any violence, without intervening directly. As you breathe out, you can gently say, "Breathing out, I know that I am breathing out."

I take care of my breath as if it were my tender little baby. I breathe in, and I let my in-breath proceed naturally. I rejoice in the fact that my breathing is there. Breathing in, I know that I am breathing in. Breathing out, I know that I am breathing out. I smile at my out-breath. This is how you can practice. You will get a great deal of joy out of it right away, and if you continue for a minute, you will see that your breathing is already different. After a minute of practicing breathing mindfully, without discrimination, the quality of your breathing improves. It becomes calmer and longer, and the gentleness and harmony generated by your breathing penetrates into your body and into your mental formations.

Try to breathe in this way when you experience joy. For example, when you are looking at a sunset and are in contact with the beauty of nature, practice mindful breathing. Touch deeply the beauty that is before you. I am breathing in—what happiness! I am breathing out—the sunset is lovely! Continue that way for a few minutes. Getting in touch with the beauty of nature makes life much more beautiful, much more real, and the more mindful and concentrated you are, the more deeply the sunset will reveal itself to you. Your happiness is multiplied by ten, by twenty. Look at a leaf or a flower with mindfulness, listen to the song of a bird, and you will get much more deeply in touch with them. After a minute of this practice, your joy will increase; your breathing will become deeper and more gentle; and this gentleness and depth will influence your body.

Mindful breathing is a kind of bridge that brings the body and the mind together. If through mindfulness of the breath you generate harmony, depth, and calm, these will penetrate into your body and mind. In fact, whatever happens in the mind affects the body, and vice versa. If you generate peacefulness in your breathing, that peacefulness permeates your body and your state of mind. If you have practiced meditation, you have already discovered this. If you have been able to embrace your in-breath and your out-breath with tenderness, you know that they in turn embrace your body and your mind. Peace is contagious. Happiness is also contagious, because in the practice of meditation, the three elements of body, mind, and breath become one.

So as you breathe in, respect the in-breath. Light up the lamp of mindfulness so that it illuminates your in-breath. "Breathing in, I know that I am breathing in." It's simple. When the in-breath is short, you take note of the fact that it is short. That's all. You don't need to judge. Just note very simply: my in-breath is short and I know that it is short. Do not try to make it longer. Let it be short. And when your in-breath is long, you simply say to yourself, "My in-breath is long."

You respect your in-breath, your out-breath, your physical body, and your mental formations. The in-breath moves inward; the out-breath moves outward. In and out. It's child's play; but it provides a great deal of happiness. During the time you are doing it, there is no tension at all. You are here for life; and if you are here for life, life will be here for you. It's simple.

WALK LIKE A BUDDHA

Walking is an important form of Buddhist meditation. It can be a very deep spiritual practice. But when the Buddha walked, he walked without effort. He just enjoyed walking. He didn't have to strain, because when you walk in mindfulness, you are in touch with the all the wonders of life within you and around you. This is the best way to practice, with the appearance of non-practice. You don't make any effort, you don't struggle, you just enjoy walking, but it's very deep. "My practice," the Buddha said, "is the practice of non-practice, the attainment of non-attainment."

For many of us, the idea of practice without effort, of the relaxed pleasure of mindfulness, seems very difficult. That is because we don't walk with our feet. Of course, physically our feet are doing the walking, but because our minds are elsewhere, we are not walking with our full body and our full consciousness. We see our minds and our bodies as two separate things. While our bodies are walking one way, our consciousness is tugging us in a different direction.

For the Buddha, mind and the body are two aspects of the same thing. Walking is as simple as putting one foot in front of the other. But we often find it difficult or tedious. We drive a few blocks rather than walk in order to "save time." When we understand the interconnectedness of our bodies and our minds, the simple act of walking like the Buddha can feel supremely easy and pleasurable.

You can make a step and touch the earth in such a way that you establish yourself in the present moment, and you will arrive in the here and the now. You don't need to make any effort at all. Your foot touches the earth mindfully, and you arrive firmly in the here and the now. And suddenly you are free—free from all projects, all worries, all expectations. You are fully present, fully alive, and you are touching the earth.

When you practice slow walking meditation alone, you may like to try this: Breathe in and take one step, and focus all your attention on the sole of your foot. If you have not arrived fully, 100 percent in the here and the now, don't make the next step. You have the luxury of doing this.

Then when you're sure that you've arrived 100 percent in the here and the now, touching reality deeply, then you smile and you make the next step. When you walk like this, you print your stability, your solidity, your freedom, your joy on the ground. Your foot is like a seal, the seal of the emperor. When you put the seal on a piece of paper, the seal makes an impression. Looking in your footstep, what do we see? We see the mark of freedom, the mark of solidity, the mark of happiness, the mark of life.

I'm sure you can make a step like that, because there is a Buddha in you. It's called buddhanature, the capacity of being aware of what is going on. What's going on is this: I am alive, I am making a step. A person, a human being, *Homo sapiens*, should be able to do this. There is a Buddha in every one of us, and we should allow the Buddha to walk.

TOUCHING THE EARTH

In the Buddhist tradition I am part of, we do a practice called "Touching the Earth" every day. It helps us in many ways. You too could be helped by doing this practice. When you feel restless or lack confidence in yourself, or when you feel angry or unhappy, you can kneel down and touch the ground deeply with your hand. Touch the Earth as if it were your favorite thing or your best friend.

The earth has been there for a long time. She is mother to all of us. She knows everything. The Buddha asked the earth to be his witness by touching her with his hand when he had some doubt and fear before his awakening. The earth appeared to him as a beautiful mother. In her arms she carried flowers and fruit, birds and butterflies, and many different animals, and offered them to the Buddha. The Buddha's doubts and fears instantly disappeared. Whenever you feel unhappy, come to the earth and ask for her help. Touch her deeply, the way the Buddha did. Suddenly, you too will see the earth with all her flowers and fruit, trees and birds, animals and all the living beings that she has produced. All these things she offers to you. You have more opportunities to be happy than you ever thought. The earth shows her love to you and her patience. The earth is very patient. She sees you suffer, she helps you, and she protects you. When we die, she takes us back into her arms.

With the earth you are very safe. She is always there, in all her wonderful expressions like trees, flowers, butterflies, and sunshine. Whenever you are tired or unhappy, Touching the Earth is a very good practice to heal you and restore your joy.

MINDFUL LIVING

When you eat your breakfast, even if it is just a small bite early in the morning, eat in such a way that freedom is possible. While eating breakfast, don't think of the future, of what you are going to do. Your practice is to simply eat breakfast. Your breakfast is there for you; you have to be there for your breakfast. You can chew each morsel of food with joy and freedom.

When I hold a piece of bread, I look at it, and sometimes I smile at it. The piece of bread is an ambassador of the cosmos offering nourishment and support. Looking deeply into the piece of bread, I see the sunshine, the clouds, the great earth. Without the sunshine, no wheat can grow. Without the clouds, there is no rain for the wheat to grow. Without the great earth, nothing can grow. That is why the piece of bread that I hold in my hand is a wonder of life. It is there for all of us. We have to be there for it.

Eat with gratitude. And when you put the piece of bread into your mouth, chew only your bread and not your projects, worries, fears, or anger. This is the practice of mindfulness. You chew mindfully and you know that you are chewing the bread, the wonderful nourishment of life. This brings you freedom and joy. Eat every morsel of your breakfast like that, not allowing yourself to be carried away from the experience of eating. This is a training.

When you brush your teeth, how much time can you afford for brushing your teeth? At least one minute, maybe two? Brush your teeth in such a way that freedom and joy are possible, not allowing yourself to be carried away by concerns about what you will do after you are done.

"I am standing here, brushing my teeth. I still have teeth to brush. I have toothpaste and a toothbrush. And my practice is to be alive, to be free to enjoy tooth-brushing." Don't allow yourself to be a slave of the past or the future. This practice is the practice of freedom. And if freedom is there, you will enjoy brushing your teeth. Resist the tendency to be carried away by your thoughts and fears.

It's interesting that in the United States you call it the restroom; do you feel restful in your restroom? In France, they used to call it *la cabine d'aisance. Aisance* means ease; you feel at ease, you feel comfortable. So when you go to the restroom, feel at ease with it, enjoy your time in the restroom. That's my practice. When I urinate, I allow myself to be entirely with the act of urinating. If you have freedom, then urinating is very pleasant. You allow yourself to invest 100 percent of your body and mind into the act of urinating. It can free you. It can be joyful.

When you drive to and from work, instead of thinking of your destination, enjoy every moment of driving. Before I begin my work of teaching, I do not bother myself with the question, "What will my friends ask and how shall I answer?" I do not bother myself with this question at all. From my room to the place where I teach, I enjoy every step and I live each moment of my walk deeply. When I arrive, I feel fresh and ready to offer my answers to questions. It is possible to enjoy mindful living during every moment of daily life.

RULING THE FIVE SKANDHAS

Each one of us is sovereign over the territory of our own being and the five elements

(Sanskrit: *skandhas*) we are made of. These elements are form (body), feelings, perceptions, mental formations, and consciousness. Our practice is to look deeply into these five elements and discover the true nature of our being—the true nature of our suffering, our happiness, our peace, our fearlessness.

But when we've abandoned our territory, we're not responsible rulers. We haven't practiced, and instead of taking care of our territory we've run away from it and allowed conflicts and disorder to arise. We're afraid to go back to our territory and face the difficulties and suffering there. Whenever we have fifteen "free" minutes, or an hour or two, we have the habit of using television, newspapers, music, conversation, or the telephone to forget and to run away from the reality of the elements that make up our being. We think, "I'm suffering too much, I have too many problems. I don't want to go back to them anymore."

We have to come back to our physical selves and put things in order. The Buddha gave us very concrete practices that show us how to do this. He was very clear that to clean up and transform the elements of our selves, we need to cultivate the energy of mindfulness. This is what will give us the strength to come back to ourselves.

The energy of mindfulness is something concrete that can be cultivated. When we practice walking mindfully, our solid, peaceful steps cultivate the energy of mindfulness and bring us back to the present moment. When we sit and follow our breathing, aware of our in- and out-breath, we are cultivating the energy of mindfulness. When we have a meal in mindfulness, we invest all our being in the present moment and are aware of our food and of those who are eating with us. We can cultivate the energy of mindfulness while we walk, while we breathe, while we work, while we wash the dishes or wash our clothes. A few days practicing like this can increase the energy of mindfulness in you, and that energy will help you, protect you, and give you courage to go back to yourself, to see and embrace what is there in your territory.

There are real, painful feelings, strong emotions, and troubling perceptions that agitate or make us afraid. With the energy of mindfulness, we can spend time with these difficult feelings without running away. We can embrace them the way a parent embraces a child and say to them, "Darling, I am here for you; I have come back; I'm going to take care of you." This is what we can do with all our emotions, feelings, and perceptions.

When you begin to practice Buddhism, you begin as a part-time Buddha and slowly you become a full-time Buddha. Sometimes you fall back and become a part-time Buddha again, but with steady practice you become a full-time Buddha again. Buddhahood is within reach because, like the Buddha, you're a human being. You can become a Buddha whenever you like; the Buddha is available in the here and now, anytime, anywhere. When you are a part-time Buddha, your romantic relationships may go well some of the time. When you are a full-time Buddha, you can find a way to be present and happy in your relationship full time, no matter what difficulties arise.

Becoming a Buddha is not so difficult. A Buddha is someone who is enlightened, capable of loving and forgiving. You know that at times you're like that. So enjoy being a Buddha. When you sit, allow the Buddha in you to sit. When you walk, allow the Buddha in you to walk. Enjoy your practice. If you don't become a Buddha, who will?

HABIT ENERGY

There is a story in Zen circles about a man and a horse. The horse is galloping quickly, and it appears that the man on the horse is going somewhere important. Another man, standing alongside the road, shouts, "Where are you going?" and the first man replies, "I don't know! Ask the horse!" This is also our story. We are riding a horse, we don't know where we are going, and we can't stop. The horse is our habit energy pulling us along, and we are powerless. We are always running, and it has become a habit. We struggle all the time even during our sleep. We are at war within ourselves, and we can easily start a war with others.

We have to learn the art of stopping— stopping our thinking, our habit energies, our forgetfulness, the strong emotions that rule us. When an emotion rushes through us like a storm, we have no peace. We turn on the TV and then we turn it off. We pick up a book and then we put it down. How can we stop this state of agitation? How can we stop our fear, despair, anger, and craving? We can stop by practicing mindful breathing, mindful talking, mindful smiling, and deep looking in order to understand. When we are mindful, touching deeply the present moment, the fruits are always understanding, acceptance, love, and the desire to relieve suffering and bring joy.

But our habit energies are often stronger than our volition. We say and do things we don't want to and afterward we regret it. We make ourselves and others suffer, and we bring about a lot of damage. We may vow not to do it again, but we do it again. Why? Because our habit energies push us.

We need the energy of mindfulness to recognize and be present with our habit energy in order to stop this course of destruction. With mindfulness, we have the capacity to recognize the habit energy every time it manifests. "Hello, my habit energy, I know you are there!" If we just smile to it, it will lose much of its strength. Mindfulness is the energy that allows us to recognize our habit energy and prevent it from dominating us.

Forgetfulness is the opposite. We drink a cup of tea, but we do not know we are drinking a cup of tea. We sit with the person we love, but we don't know that she is there. We walk, but we are not really walking. We are someplace else, thinking about the past or the future. The horse of our habit energy is carrying us along, and we are its captive. We need to stop our horse and reclaim our liberty. We need to shine the light of mindfulness on everything we do, so the darkness of forgetfulness will disappear.

DARKNESS BECOMES LIGHT

Observe the changes that take place in your mind under the light of awareness. Even your breathing has changed and become "not-two" (I don't want to say "one") with your observing self. This is also true of your thoughts and feelings, which, together with their effects, are suddenly transformed. When you do not try to judge or suppress them, they become intertwined with the observing mind.

From time to time you may become restless, and the restlessness will not go away. At such times, just sit quietly, follow your breathing, smile a half-smile, and shine your awareness on the restlessness. Don't judge it or try to destroy it, because this restlessness is you yourself. It is born, has some period of existence, and fades away, quite naturally. Don't be in too big a hurry to find its source. Don't try too hard to make it disappear. Just illuminate it. You will see that little by little it will change, merge, become connected with you, the observer. Any psychological state that you subject to this illumination will eventually soften and acquire the same nature as the observing mind.

Throughout your meditation, keep the sun of your awareness shining. Like the physical sun, which lights every leaf and every blade of grass, our awareness lights our every thought and feeling, allowing us to recognize them, be aware of their birth, duration, and dissolution, without judging or evaluating, welcoming or banishing them. It is important that you do not consider awareness to be your "ally," called on to suppress the "enemies" that are your unruly thoughts. Do not turn your mind into a battlefield. Do not have a war there; for *all* your feelings—joy, sorrow, anger, hatred—are part of yourself. Awareness is like an elder brother or sister, gentle and attentive, who is there to guide and enlighten. It is a tolerant and lucid presence, never violent or discriminating. It is there to recognize and identify thoughts and feelings, not to judge them as good or bad, or place them into opposing camps in order to fight with each other. Opposition between good and bad is often compared to light and dark, but if we look at it in a different way, we will see that when light shines, darkness does not disappear. It doesn't leave; it merges with the light. It becomes the light.

To meditate does not mean to fight with a problem. To meditate means to observe. Your smile proves it. It proves that you are being gentle with yourself, that the sun of awareness is shining in you, that you have control of your situation. You are yourself, and you have acquired some peace. It is this peace that makes a child love to be near you.

A DAY OF MINDFULNESS

Every day and every hour, one should practice mindfulness. That's easy to say, but to carry it out in practice is not. That's why I suggest that each person should try hard to reserve one day out of the week to devote entirely to their practice of mindfulness. In principle, of course, every day should be your day, and every hour your hour. But the fact is that very few of us have reached such a point. We have the impression that our family, place of work, and society rob us of all our time. So I urge that everyone set aside one day each week.

If it is Saturday, then Saturday must be entirely your day, a day during which you are completely the master. Then Saturday will be the lever that will lift you to the habit of practicing mindfulness. Every worker in a peace or service community, no matter how urgent its work, has the right to such a day, for without it we will lose ourselves quickly in a life full of worry and action, and our responses will become increasingly useless. Whatever the day chosen, it can be considered as the day of mindfulness.

To set up a day of mindfulness, figure out a way to remind yourself at the moment of waking that this day is your day of mindfulness. You might hang something on the ceiling or on the wall, a paper with the word "mindfulness," or a pine branch—anything that will suggest to you as you open your eyes and see it that today is your day of mindfulness. Today is your day. Remembering that, perhaps you can feel a smile which affirms that you are in complete mindfulness, a smile which nourishes that perfect mindfulness.

While still lying in bed, begin slowly to follow your breath—slow, long, and conscious breaths. Then slowly rise from bed (instead of turning out all at once as usual), nourishing mindfulness by every motion. Once up, brush your teeth, wash your face, and do all your morning activities in a calm and relaxing way, each movement done in mindfulness. Follow your breath, take hold of it, and don't let your thoughts scatter. Each movement should be done calmly. Measure your steps with quiet, long breaths. Maintain a half smile.

Spend at least a half hour taking a bath. Bathe slowly and mindfully, so that by the time you have finished, you feel light and refreshed. Afterward, you might do household work such as washing dishes, dusting and wiping off tables, scrubbing the kitchen floor, or arranging books on their shelves. Whatever the tasks, do them slowly and with ease, in mindfulness. Don't do any task in order to get it over with. Resolve to do each job in a relaxed way, with all your attention. Enjoy and be one with your work. Without this, the day of mindfulness will be of no value at all. The feeling that any task is a nuisance will soon disappear if it is done in mindfulness. Take the example of the Zen masters. No matter what task or motion they undertake, they do it slowly and evenly, without reluctance.

For those who are just beginning to practice, it is best to maintain a spirit of silence throughout the day. That doesn't mean that on the day of mindfulness, you shouldn't speak at all. You can talk, you can even go ahead and sing, but if you talk or sing, do it in complete mindfulness of what you are saying or singing, and keep talking and singing to a minimum. Naturally, it is

THE POCKET THICH NHAT HANH

possible to sing and practice mindfulness at the same time, just as long as one is conscious of the fact that one is singing and aware of what one is singing. But be warned that it is much easier, when singing or talking, to stray from mindfulness if your meditation strength is still weak.

At lunchtime, prepare a meal for yourself. Cook the meal and wash the dishes in mindfulness. In the morning, after you have cleaned and straightened up your house, and in the afternoon, after you have worked in the garden or watched clouds or gathered flowers, prepare a pot of tea to sit and drink in mindfulness. Allow yourself a good length of time to do this. Don't drink your tea like someone who gulps down a cup of coffee during a work break. Drink your tea slowly and reverently, as if it is the axis on which the whole earth revolves— slowly, evenly, without rushing toward the future. Live the actual moment. Only this moment is life. Don't be attached to the future. Don't worry about things you have to do. Don't think about getting up or taking off to do anything.

In the evening, you might read scripture and copy passages, write letters to friends, or do anything else you enjoy outside of your normal duties during the week. But whatever you do, do it in mindfulness. Eat only a little for the evening meal. Later, around ten or eleven o'clock, as you sit in meditation, you will be able to sit more easily on an empty stomach. Afterward you might take a slow walk in the fresh night air, following your breath in mindfulness and measuring the length of your breaths by your steps. Finally, return to your room and sleep in mindfulness.

Such a day of mindfulness is crucial. Its effect on the other days of the week is immeasurable. After only three months of observing such a day of mindfulness once a week, I know that you will see a significant change in your life. The day of mindfulness will begin to penetrate the other days of the week, enabling you to eventually live seven days a week in mindfulness. I'm sure you agree with me on the day of mindfulness's importance!

·2

ENLIGHTENMENT

INTERBEING

If you are a poet, you will see clearly that there is a cloud floating in this sheet of paper. Without a cloud, there will be no rain; without rain, the trees cannot grow; and without trees, we cannot make paper. The cloud is essential for the paper to exist. If the cloud is not here, the sheet of paper cannot be here either. So we can say that the cloud and the paper "inter-are."

"Interbeing" is a word that is not in the dictionary yet, but if we combine the prefix "inter-" with the verb "to be," we have a new verb, "inter-be." If we look into this sheet of paper even more deeply, we can see the sunshine in it. If the sunshine is not there, the forest cannot grow. In fact, nothing can grow. Even we cannot grow without sunshine. And so, we know that the sunshine is also in this sheet of paper. The paper and the sunshine inter-are. And if we continue to look, we can see the logger who cut the tree and brought it to the mill to be transformed into paper. And we see the wheat. We know that the logger cannot exist without his daily bread, and therefore the wheat that became his bread is also in this sheet of paper. And the logger's father and mother are in it too. When we look in this way, we see that without all of these things, this sheet of paper cannot exist.

Looking even more deeply, we can see we are in it too. This is not difficult to see, because when we look at a sheet of paper, the sheet of paper is part of our perception. Your mind is in here and mine is also. So we can say that everything is in here in this sheet of paper. You cannot point out one thing that is not here—time, space, the earth, the rain, the minerals in the soil, the sunshine, the cloud, the river, the heat. Everything coexists with this sheet of paper. That is why I think the word inter-be should be in the dictionary. To be is to inter-be. You cannot just *be* by yourself alone. You have to inter-be with every other thing. This sheet of paper is, because everything else is.

Suppose we try to return one of the elements to its source. Suppose we return the sunshine to the sun. Do you think that this sheet of paper would be possible? No, without sunshine nothing can be. And if we return the logger to his mother, then we have no sheet of paper either. The fact is that this sheet of paper is made up only of "non-paper elements." And if we return these non-paper elements to their sources, then there can be no paper at all. Without non-paper elements, like mind, logger, sunshine, and so on, there will be no paper. As thin as this sheet of paper is, it contains everything in the universe in it.

THE BUDDHA

Buddha was not a god. He was a human being like you and me, and he suffered just as we do. If we go to the Buddha with our hearts open, he will look at us, his eyes filled with compassion, and say, "Because there is suffering in your heart, it is possible for you to enter my heart."

The layman Vimalakirti said, "Because the world is sick, I am sick. Because people suffer, I have to suffer." This statement was also made by the Buddha. Please don't think that because you are unhappy, because there is pain in your heart, that you cannot go to the Buddha. It is exactly because there is pain in your heart that communication is possible. Your suffering and my suffering are the basic condition for us to enter the Buddha's heart, and for the Buddha to enter our hearts.

For forty-five years, the Buddha said, over and over again, "I teach only suffering and the transformation of suffering." When we recognize and acknowledge our own suffering, the Buddha—which means the Buddha in us—will look at it, discover what has brought it about, and prescribe a course of action that can transform it into peace, joy, and liberation. Suffering is the means the Buddha used to liberate himself, and it is also the means by which we can become free.

The ocean of suffering is immense, but if you turn around, you can see the land. The seed of suffering in you may be strong, but don't wait until you have no more suffering before allowing yourself to be happy. When one tree in the garden is sick, you have to care for it. But don't overlook all the healthy trees. Even while you have pain in your heart, you can enjoy the many wonders of life—the beautiful sunset, the smile of a child, the many flowers and trees. To suffer is not enough. Please don't be imprisoned by your suffering.

If you have experienced hunger, you know that having food is a miracle. If you have suffered from the cold you know the preciousness of warmth. When you have suffered, you know how to appreciate the elements of paradise that are present. Don't ignore your suffering, but don't forget to enjoy the wonders of life, for your sake and for the benefit of many beings.

I grew up in a time of war. There was destruction all around—children, adults, values, a whole country. As a young person, I suffered a lot. Once the door of awareness has been opened, you cannot close it. The wounds of war in me are still not all healed. There are nights I lie awake and embrace my people, my country, and the whole planet with my mindful breathing.

Without suffering, you cannot grow. Without suffering, you cannot get the peace and joy you deserve. Please don't run away from your suffering. Embrace it and cherish it. Go to the Buddha, sit with him, and show him your pain. He will look at you with loving-kindness, compassion, and mindfulness, and show you ways to embrace your suffering and look deeply into it. With understanding and compassion, you will be able to heal the wounds in your heart, and the wounds in the world. The Buddha called suffering a Noble Truth, because our suffering has the capacity of showing us the path to liberation. Embrace your suffering, and let it reveal to you the way to peace.

IMPERMANENCE

The Buddha taught that everything is impermanent—flowers, tables, mountains, political regimes, bodies, feelings, perceptions, mental formations, and consciousness. We cannot find anything that is permanent. Flowers decompose, but knowing this does not prevent us from loving flowers. In fact, we are able to love them more because we know how to treasure them while they are still alive. If we learn to look at a flower in a way that impermanence is revealed to us, when it dies, we will not suffer. Impermanence is more than an idea. It is a practice to help us touch reality.

When we study impermanence, we have to ask, "Is there anything in this teaching that has to do with my daily life, my daily difficulties, my suffering?" If we see impermanence as merely a philosophy, it is not the Buddha's teaching. Every time we look or listen, the object of our perception can reveal to us the nature of impermanence. We have to nourish our insight into impermanence all day long.

When we look deeply into impermanence, we see that things change because causes and conditions change. When we look deeply into nonself, we see that the existence of every single thing is possible only because of the existence of everything else. We see that everything else is the cause and condition for its existence. We see that everything else is in it.

From the point of view of time, we say "impermanence," and from the point of view of space, we say "nonself." Things cannot remain themselves for two consecutive moments; therefore, there is nothing that can be called a permanent "self." Before you entered this room, you were different physically and mentally. Looking deeply at impermanence, you see nonself. Looking deeply at nonself, you see impermanence. We cannot say, "I can accept impermanence, but nonself is too difficult." They are the same.

Understanding impermanence can give us confidence, peace, and joy. Impermanence does not necessarily lead to suffering. Without impermanence, life could not be. Without impermanence, your daughter could not grow up into a beautiful young lady. Without impermanence, oppressive political regimes would never change. We think impermanence makes us suffer. The Buddha gave the example of a dog that was hit by a stone and got angry at the stone. It is not impermanence that makes us suffer. What makes us suffer is wanting things to be permanent when they are not.

We need to learn to appreciate the value

of impermanence. If we are in good health and are aware of impermanence, we will take good care of ourselves. When we know that the person we love is impermanent, we will cherish our beloved all the more. Impermanence teaches us to respect and value every moment and all the precious things around us and inside of us. When we practice mindfulness of impermanence, we become fresher and more loving.

Looking deeply can become a way of life. We can practice conscious breathing to help us be in touch with things and to look deeply at their impermanent nature. This practice will keep us from complaining that everything is impermanent and therefore not worth living for. Impermanence is what makes transformation possible. We should learn to say, "Long live impermanence." Thanks to impermanence, we can change suffering into joy.

DEEP SEEING

Being in contact with life in the present moment, we observe deeply what is. Then we are able to see the impermanent and selfless nature of all that is. Impermanence and selflessness are not negative aspects of life but the very foundations on which life is built. Impermanence is the constant transformation of things. Without impermanence, there can be no life. Selflessness is the interdependent nature of all things. Without interdependence, nothing could exist. Without the sun, the clouds, and the Earth, the tulip could not be. We often feel sad about the impermanence and selflessness of life, because we forget that, without impermanence and selflessness, life cannot be. To be aware of impermanence and selflessness does not take away the joy of being alive. On the contrary, it adds healthiness, stability, and freedom. It is because people cannot see the impermanent and selfless nature of things that they suffer. They take what is impermanent as permanent and that what is selfless as having a self.

Looking deeply into a rose, we can see its impermanent nature quite clearly. At the same time, we can still see its beauty and value its preciousness. Because we perceive its fragile and impermanent nature, we may see that flower as even more beautiful and precious. The more fragile something is, the more beautiful and precious it is—for example, a rainbow, a sunset, a cereus cactus flowering by night, a falling star. Looking at the sun rising over Vulture Peak, at the town of Vesali, at a field of ripe, golden rice, the Buddha saw their beauty and told Ananda so.

Seeing deeply the impermanent nature of those beautiful things, their transformation and disappearance, the Buddha did not suffer or despair. We, too, by observing deeply and seeing impermanence and selflessness in all that is, can overcome despair and suffering and experience the preciousness of the miracles of everyday life—a glass of clear water, a cool breeze, a step taken in ease and freedom. All these are wonderful things, although they are impermanent and selfless.

Life is suffering, but it is also wonderful. Sickness, old age, death, accident, starvation, unemployment, and natural disasters cannot be avoided in life. But, if our understanding is deep and our mind free, we can accept these things with tranquility, and the suffering will already be greatly lessened. This is not to say we should close our eyes before suffering. By being in contact with suffering, we give rise to and nourish our natural love and compassion. Suffering becomes the element that nourishes our love and compassion, and so we are not afraid of it. When our heart is filled with love and compassion, we will act in ways to help relieve the sufferings of others.

If the human species has been able to make any progress, it is because of our heart of love and compassion. We need to learn from compassionate beings how to develop the practice of deep observation for the sake of others. Then others will be able to learn from us the way to live in the present and see the impermanent and self-less nature of all that is. This insight will lighten suffering.

Fear of the unexpected leads many people to live a constricted and anxious life. No one can know in advance the misfortunes that may happen to us and our loved ones, but if we learn to live in an awakened way, living deeply every moment of our life, treating those who are close to us with gentleness and understanding, then we will have nothing to regret when something happens to us or to them. Living in the present moment, we are able to be in touch with life's wonderful, refreshing, and health-giving phenomena, which allow us to heal the wounds in ourselves. Every day we become more wonderful, fresh, and healthy.

NOTHING TO ATTAIN

There is nothing to do, nothing to realize, no program, no agenda. This is the Buddhist teaching about eschatology. Does the rose have *to do* something? No, the purpose of a rose it *to be* a rose. Your purpose is to be yourself. You don't have to run anywhere to become someone else. You are wonderful just as you are. This teaching of the Buddha allows us to enjoy ourselves, the blue sky, and everything that is refreshing and healing in the present moment.

There is no need to put anything in front of us and run after it. We already have everything we are looking for, everything we want to become. We are already a Buddha, so why not just take the hand of another Buddha and practice walking meditation? This is the teaching of the *Avatamsaka Sutra*. Be yourself. Life is precious as it is. All the elements for your happiness are already here. There is no need to run, strive, search, or struggle. Just be. Just being in the moment in this place is the deepest practice of meditation. Most people cannot believe that just walking as though you have nowhere to go is enough. They think that striving and competing are normal and necessary. Try practicing aimlessness for just five minutes, and you will see how happy you are during those five minutes.

The *Heart Sutra* says that there is "nothing to attain." We meditate not to attain enlightenment, because enlightenment is already in us. We don't have to search anywhere. We don't need a purpose or a goal. We don't practice in order to obtain some high position. In aimlessness, we see that we do not lack anything, that we already are what we want to become, and our striving just comes to a halt. We are at peace in the present moment, just seeing the sunlight streaming through our window or hearing the sound of the rain. We don't have to run after anything. We can enjoy every moment. People talk about entering nirvana, but we are already there. Aimlessness and nirvana are one.

BEYOND BIRTH
AND DEATH

It is our idea of birth and death that takes away our peace and happiness in everyday life. And it is meditation that will rid us of the fear that is born from the idea of birth and death. This is the virtue of deep looking in meditation. It helps you to see the heart of reality very deeply. To touch the nature of interbeing is to touch the very nature of no-death and no-birth.

The notion of death, of nothingness, is very dangerous. It makes people suffer a lot. In Buddhist teaching nothingness is only a concept, and it is never applicable to reality. The Buddha said, "When conditions are sufficient, the thing manifests, and when they are not sufficient, the thing remains hidden." There is neither birth nor death. There is only manifestation, appearance. Concepts like birth and death, being and nonbeing, are not applicable to reality. The wave on the water is free from birth and death. It is free from being and nonbeing. The wave is the wave.

The word "suchness" describes reality as it is. Concepts and ideas are incapable of expressing reality as it is. Nirvana, the ultimate reality, cannot be described, because it is free of all concepts and ideas. Nirvana is the extinction of all concepts. It is total freedom. Most of our suffering arises from our ideas and concepts. If you are able to free yourself from these concepts, anxiety and fear will disappear. Nirvana, the ultimate reality, or God, is of the nature of no-birth and no-death. It is total freedom. We need to touch this reality to leave behind the fear connected with the idea of birth and death.

We are afraid of nonbeing. "I am somebody, I am something," we feel. "Today I am, and I am afraid that one day I will no longer be." But it is impossible for being to become nonbeing. The Buddha said it in absolutely simple terms: "This is, because that is." This refers to the manifestation of phenomena on the basis of the law of inter-dependent origination. When conditions are sufficient, there is a manifestation. You could call that "being," but that would be inaccurate. In the same way, you could call the situation before manifestation arises "nonbeing," but that is equally incorrect. The situation is simply one of manifestation or non-manifestation.

Just because something is not visibly manifest, you cannot say that it is nonexistent, just so much nothing. In April at Plum Village, you do not see sunflowers. The hills are not covered with their blossoms, but you cannot say that there are no sunflowers. The sunflowers are hidden in the earth; they are just lacking one of the conditions for their manifestation, sunshine. It is false to say that the sunflowers do not exist.

So what is death? It is simply the cessation of manifestation, followed by other forms of manifestation. In wintertime, we do not see dragonflies or butterflies. So we think that everything is dead. But suddenly spring comes, and the dragonflies and butterflies manifest again. That which is currently not perceivable is not nonexistent. But we cannot say that it is existent either.

Existence and nonexistence are just concepts. There is only manifestation and non-manifestation, which depend on our perception. If you have perception that is deep enough, a deep insight into life, then you are free from all these concepts such as being and nonbeing, birth and death. This is the highest level of the Buddha's teaching. You are looking for relief for your pain; but the greatest relief that you can ever obtain comes from touching the nature of no-birth and no-death.

PURE LAND

We all know that the wonders of life are always there—the blue sky, the white cloud, the beautiful river, the rain, the flowers, the birds, the trees, the children. Yesterday during walking meditation I saw two little violet flowers in the grass. They were so beautiful, tiny, very well manifested, and I picked one and I picked the other, and I offered them to two venerable monks who had come to visit from Vietnam. I told them, "These flowers are available only in the Pure Land," and I am sure that the venerables understood the message. Because if we are mindful, if we can touch the wonders of life deeply, then the

Pure Land, the Kingdom of God, is available to us.

The fact is that the Pure Land is always available. The question remains: are we available to the Pure Land? To make ourselves available to the Pure Land is not difficult at all. Become mindful while you look, while you touch, while you touch the earth with your feet. It is possible for us to stay in the Pure Land twenty-four hours a day, with the condition that we keep mindfulness alive in us.

There is a tendency to believe that this land is full of misery, and we want to go somewhere where there is no suffering. My definition of the Pure Land, or the Kingdom of God, is not a place where there is no suffering, because suffering and happiness inter-are. Happiness can only be recognized against the background of suffering. So we need suffering in order to recognize happiness. Looking deeply we know that happiness is not possible when we don't have understanding and compassion in us. A happy person is a person who has a lot of understanding and compassion. Without compassion and understanding you cannot relate to anyone, and you are totally isolated. Please observe and look around you and you will see that very well: the person who is full of understanding and compassion, that person does not suffer; he or she is happy. To be really happy, we should cultivate understanding and compassion. But if suffering is not there, it is impossible to cultivate understanding and compassion. It is by getting in touch with the suffering that understanding arises and compassion arises. Imagine a place where there is no suffering. Our children would have no chance to develop their understanding, to learn how to be compassionate.

It is by touching suffering that one learns to understand and to be compassionate. If in the Kingdom of God there is no suffering, there will be no understanding and compassion either, and without that you cannot call it the Kingdom of God or the Pure Land of the Buddha. This is something very clear, very simple. So my definition of the Pure Land of the Buddha, the Kingdom of God, is the place where there are plenty of opportunities for you to learn to be understanding and to be compassionate. When you have a lot of understanding and compassion, you are no longer afraid of suffering.

It is like when you are a good organic gardener, you are no longer afraid of the garbage, because you know how to transform the garbage. That is the nondualistic way of seeing things. The little flowers I picked yesterday, and offered to the venerables from Vietnam, are wonders. If we are not mindful, we cannot get in touch with them. The wonders of life are there, right in the present moment inside of us and around us. Our brain is a wonder. Our eyes are a wonder. Our heart is a wonder. Every cell of our body is a wonder. And around us everything is a wonder. All these things belong to the Kingdom of God, to the Pure Land of the Buddha. But we have lived in such a way that we totally ignore their presence. We get caught in our worries, in our despair, in our jealousy, in our fear, and we lose the Kingdom, we lose the Pure Land.

THE TWO DIMENSIONS

The first dimension is that of history, the events we experience and what we can see and know in our own lifetimes. The second dimension is that of ultimate reality, which goes beyond time and space. Everything, all phenomena, participate in these two dimensions. When we look at a wave on the surface of the ocean, we can see the form of the wave and we locate the wave in space and time. Space and time are not two separate entities; space is made of time and time is made of space. Looking at a wave from the perspective of the historical dimension, it seems to have a beginning and an end, a birth and a death. A wave can be high or low, a wave can be long or short—many qualities can be ascribed to the wave. The notions of "birth" and "death," "high" and "low," "beginning" and "ending," "coming" and "going," "being" and "nonbeing"—all of these can be applied to a wave in the historical dimension.

We, too, are subject to these notions. When we look in terms of the historical dimension we see that we are subject to being and nonbeing. We are born, but later on we will die. We have a beginning and an end. We have come from somewhere, and we will go somewhere. That is the historical dimension. All of us belong to this dimension. Shakyamuni Buddha also has a historical dimension—he was a human being who was born in Kapilavastu and died in Kushinagara, and during his lifetime of eighty years he taught the Dharma.

At the same time, all beings and things also belong to the ultimate dimension, the dimension of reality that is not subject to notions of space and time, birth and death, coming and going. A wave is a wave, but at the same time it is water. The wave does not have to die in order to become water; it is already water right in the present moment. We don't speak of water in terms of being or nonbeing, coming and going—water is always water. To talk about a wave, we need these notions: the wave arises and passes away; it comes from somewhere or has gone somewhere; the wave has a beginning and an end; it is high or low, more or less beautiful than other waves; the wave is subject to birth and death. None of these distinctions can be applied to the wave in its ultimate dimension as water. In fact, you cannot separate the wave from its ultimate dimension.

Even though we are used to seeing everything in terms of the historical dimension, we can touch the ultimate dimension. So our practice is to become like a wave—while living the life of a wave in the historical dimension, we realize that we are also water and live the life of water. That is the essence of the practice. Because if you know your true nature of no coming, no going; no being, no nonbeing; no birth, no death, then you will have no fear and can dwell in the ultimate dimension, nirvana, right here and now. You don't have to die in order to reach nirvana. When you dwell in your true nature, you are already dwelling in nirvana. We have our historical dimension, but we also have our ultimate dimension, just as the Buddha does.

HIDE AND SEEK

One day while practicing walking meditation in the Upper Hamlet of Plum Village, I looked down and saw that I was about to step on a golden yellow leaf. It was in the autumn, when the golden leaves are very beautiful. When I saw that beautiful golden leaf, I did not want to step on it and so I hesitated briefly. But then I smiled and thought, "This leaf is only pretending to be gold, pretending to fall from the tree."

In terms of the historical dimension, that leaf was born on a branch as a new green bud in the spring, had clung to that branch for many months, changed color in autumn, and one day when a cold wind blew, it fell to the ground. But looking deeply into its ultimate dimension, we can see that the leaf is only pretending to be born, to exist for a while, and to grow old and die. The teachings of interdependence and no-self reveal to us the true unborn and undying nature of all phenomena. One day that leaf will pretend to be born again on the branch of another tree, but she is really just playing a game of hide and seek with us.

We are also playing a game of hide and seek with one another. It is not only the Buddha who pretends to be born and to enter nirvana; we also pretend to be born, to live for a while, and to pass away. You may think that your mother has passed away and is no longer here with you. But her passing away was just a pretense, and one day, when the causes and conditions are sufficient, she will reappear in one form or another. If you have enough insight you will be able to recognize your mother in her other forms. We need to look deeply into all those we love and recognize their true nature. We love our teacher, our father and mother, our children, our brothers and sisters, and when someone we love passes away, we feel great sorrow and believe we have lost that person. But ultimately nothing is lost. The true nature of those we love is unborn and undying. If we can be in touch with the ultimate dimension, we shall smile with the yellow leaf, just as we can smile at all the other changes that take place in our lives.

NO FEAR

When we look deeply into our fear, we see the desire for permanence. We're afraid of change. Our anger, our fear, our despair are born from our wrong perceptions, from our notions of being and nonbeing, coming and going, rising and falling. If we practice looking deeply, we find out that these notions cannot be applied to reality. We can touch our true nature, we can touch the ultimate dimension, and this brings about non-fear. When we trust that insight of no-birth and no-death, joy becomes possible every moment of our lives.

Visualize a cloud floating in the sky. The cloud doesn't want to change. She is afraid of dying, of becoming nothing, and that is what makes the cloud suffer. But if the cloud practices looking deeply, she will find out that it's impossible for a cloud to die. A cloud can be transformed into rain or snow or ice, but a cloud cannot become nothing; it's impossible. When the cloud has found her nature of no-death, she loses her fear. She comes to understand that to be a cloud floating in the sky is wonderful, but to be rain or snow falling on the earth is equally wonderful. So she's no longer a victim of her fear, because she's practiced looking deeply and touched her nature of deathlessness. Nothing can die. You cannot reduce being into nonbeing. Life is a process of change. Without changing, life is impossible. Once you accept that with joy, there is no fear. That is the practice of looking deeply.

THE ZEN MASTER

To return to our true home, to see into our own nature, is the aim of practice. We see into our own nature by bringing light to each act of our existence, living in a way that mindfulness is present all of the time.

When walking past the cypress tree in the courtyard, we really see it. If we do not see the cypress in our own garden, how can we expect to see into our own true nature?

A Zen master who has attained awakening is someone whose eyes are open to living reality. She is someone who, after being lost in the world of concepts, has returned home to see the cypress in the courtyard and her own nature. Hence, she cannot allow her disciple to continue to wander in the world of concepts and waste his life, his own awakening. This is why the master feels compassion every time her disciple asks a question about some Buddhist principles, such as *dharmakaya, tathata,* and the like. "This young man," she thinks, "still wishes to engage in the search for reality through concepts." And she does her best to extricate the student from the world of ideas and put him in the world of living reality. Look at the cypress in the courtyard! *Look at the cypress in the courtyard!*

One day a monk asked Chao-Chou to speak to him about Zen. Chao-Chou asked, "Have you finished your breakfast?" "Yes, master, I have eaten my breakfast." "Then go and wash your bowl."

"Go and wash your bowl." This is the same as saying, "Go and live a realized life." Instead of giving the student some explanations about Zen, the master opened the door and invited the young man to enter the world of reality. "Go and wash your bowl." These words contain no secret meaning to explore or explain. They are a simple, direct, and clear declaration. There is no enigma here, nor is this a symbol. It refers to a very concrete fact.

THREE DOORS OF LIBERATION

There is a famous Zen koan: what was your face before you were born? Contemplating this is meant to help us realize the no-birth, no-death nature of reality and of ourselves. The eighteenth-century French scientist Antoine-Laurent Lavoisier said, "Nothing is born. Nothing dies." He was not a Buddhist but a scientist looking deeply into the nature of reality, and he discovered this truth. The *Heart Sutra* also says, "No birth, no death, no production, no destruction." If you have never been born, how can you die? Grasping and rejecting are only possible when you have not seen into the heart of reality.

We usually try to hold on to life and run away from death. But, according to the teaching, everything has been nirvana from the non-beginning. So why do we have to grasp one thing and avoid another? In the ultimate dimension, there is no beginning and no end. We think there is something to attain, something outside of ourselves, but everything is already here. When we transcend notions of inside and outside, we know that the object we wish to attain is already within us. We don't have to search for it in space or time. It is already available in the present moment. The contemplation on non-attainment is very important. The object we wish to attain already is attained. We don't need to attain anything. We already have it. We already are it.

The teaching of non-attainment is developed from the teaching of aimlessness. The teaching of the Three Doors of Liberation is common to all the Buddhist schools. The first door is emptiness. Everything is empty. Empty of what? Empty of a separate self. A flower is full of everything in the cosmos—sunshine, clouds, air, and space. It is empty of only one thing, a separate existence. That is the meaning of emptiness. We can use this as a key to unlock the door to reality.

The second door is signlessness. If you see a flower only as a flower and don't see the sunshine, clouds, earth, time, and space in it, you are caught in the sign of the flower. But when you have touched the nature of interbeing of the flower, you truly see the flower. If you see a person and don't also see his society, education, ancestors, culture, and environment, you have not really seen that person. Instead, you have been taken in by the sign of that person, the outward appearance of a separate self. When you can see that person deeply, you touch the whole cosmos and you will not be fooled by appearances. This is called signlessness.

The third door is aimlessness. We already are what we want to become. We don't have to become someone else. All we have to do is be ourselves, fully and authentically. We don't have to run after anything. We already contain the whole cosmos. We simply return to ourselves through mindfulness and touch the peace and joy that are already present within us and all around us. I have arrived. I am already home. There is nothing to do. This is the third key for unlocking reality. Aimlessness, non-attainment, is a wonderful practice.

Our afflictions are none other than enlightenment. We can ride the waves of birth and death in peace. We can travel in the boat of compassion on the ocean of delusion with a smile of non-fear. In the light of interbeing, we see the flower in the garbage and the garbage in the flower. It is on the very ground of suffering, the ground of afflictions, that we can contemplate enlightenment and well-being. It is exactly in the muddy water that the lotus grows and blooms.

Bodhisattvas are those who have penetrated into the reality of no-birth and no-death. That is why they are fearless, day and night. With that freedom, they can do a lot to help those who are suffering. We can become a Buddha only by being in the world of suffering and afflictions. And when we are free, we can ride on the waves of birth and death without fear, helping those who are drowning in the ocean of suffering.

THE BUSINESSLESS PERSON

Master Linji (Japanese: Rinzai) invented the term the "businessless person," the person who has nothing to do and nowhere to go. This was his ideal example of what a person could be. In Theravada Buddhism, the ideal person was the arhat, someone who practiced to attain enlightenment. In Mahayana Buddhism, the ideal person was the bodhisattva, a compassionate being who, on the path of enlightenment, helped others. According to Master Linji, the businessless person is someone who doesn't run after enlightenment or grasp at anything, even if that thing is the Buddha. This person has simply stopped. She is no longer caught by anything, even theories or teachings. The businessless person is the true person inside each one of us.

This is the essential teaching of Master Linji. When we learn to stop and be truly alive in the present moment, we are in touch with what's going on within and around us. We aren't carried away by the past, the future, our thinking, ideas, emotions, and projects. Often we think that our ideas about things are the reality of that thing. Our notion of the Buddha may just be an idea and may be far from reality. The Buddha outside ourselves was a human being who was born, lived, and died. For us to seek such a Buddha would be to seek a shadow, a ghost Buddha, and at some point our idea of Buddha would become an obstacle for us.

Master Linji said that when we meet the ghost Buddha, we should cut off his head. Whether we're looking inside or outside ourselves, we need to cut off the head of whatever we meet, and abandon the views and ideas we have about things, including our ideas about Buddhism and Buddhist teachings. Buddhist teachings are not exalted words and scriptures existing outside us, sitting on a high shelf in the temple, but are medicine for our ills. Buddhist teachings are skillful means to cure our ignorance, craving, and anger, as well as our habit of seeking things outside and not having confidence in ourselves.

Insight can't be found in sutras, commentaries, or Dharma talks. Liberation and awakened understanding can't be found by devoting ourselves to the study of the Buddhist scriptures. This is like hoping to find fresh water in dry bones. Returning to the present moment, using our clear mind that exists right here and now, we can be in touch with liberation and enlightenment, as well as with the Buddha and all his disciples as living realities right in this moment. The person who has nothing to do is sovereign of herself. She doesn't need to put on airs or leave any trace behind. The true person is an active participant, engaged in her environment while remaining unoppressed by it. Although all phenomena are going through the various appearances of birth, abiding, changing, and dying, the true person doesn't become a victim of sadness, happiness, love, or hate. She lives in awareness as an ordinary person, whether standing, walking, lying down, or sitting. She doesn't act a part, even the part of a great Zen master. This is what Master Linji means by "be sovereign wherever you are and use that place as your seat of awakening."

SMILE OF THE BODHISATTVA

Bodhisattvas dwell on the same ground as the rest of us—the world of birth and death, permanence, and self. But thanks to the practice of looking deeply into impermanence and nonself, they are in touch with the ultimate dimension, free from the fears associated with ideas of existence and nonexistence, one and many, coming and going, birth and death. In this freedom, they ride the waves of birth and death in perfect peace. They are able to remain in the world of waves while abiding in the nature of water.

"Riding the waves of birth and death" is a description of the bodhisattvas in the *Lotus Sutra*—Avalokiteshvara, Samantabhadra, Bhaishajyaraja, and Gadgadasvara—who demonstrate the practice in this life. This is the dimension of action. In a world of pain and grief, these bodhisattvas are still able to smile with compassion and fearlessness, because they are able to see the nonduality of afflictions and awakening and touch the reality of nirvana. Buddhist texts speak of three kinds of gifts—material resources, sharing the Dharma with others, and non-fear, which is the greatest gift. Because bodhisattvas are free from fear, they can help many people. Non-fear is the greatest gift we can offer to those we love. Nothing is more precious. But we cannot offer that gift unless we ourselves have it. If we have practiced and have touched the ultimate dimension of reality, we too can smile the bodhisattvas' smile of non-fear. Like them, we don't need to run away from our afflictions. We don't need to go somewhere else to attain enlightenment.

We see that afflictions and enlightenment are one. When we have a deluded mind, we see only afflictions. But when we have a true mind, the afflictions are no longer there. There is only enlightenment. We are no longer afraid of birth and death because we have touched the nature of interbeing. Those who work with the dying especially need to practice solidity and non-fear. Others need our stability and non-fear in order to be able to die peacefully. If we know how to touch the ultimate dimension of reality, if we know the reality of no-birth and no-death, we can transcend all fear. Then, when we are sitting with a dying person, we can be a source of comfort and inspiration to them. Non-fear is the greatest practice in Buddhism. To free ourselves from all fear we must touch the ground of our being and train ourselves to look directly into the light of compassion.

The *Heart Sutra* describes how the bodhisattva Avalokiteshvara, because he is able to look deeply into the nonself nature of the five aggregates (skandhas), discovers the nature of emptiness and immediately overcomes all afflictions. From this he receives the energy of non-fear, which is why he is able to help so many others. Once we have seen that our afflictions are no other than enlightenment, we too can ride joyfully on the waves of birth and death.

A gardener does not chase after flowers and try to run away from garbage. She accepts both, and she takes good care of both. She is not attached to either nor does she reject either, because she sees that the nature of both is interbeing. She has made peace with the flower and the garbage. A bodhisattva handles enlightenment and afflictions in the same way a skillful gardener handles flowers and garbage—without discrimination. She knows how to do the work of transformation, and so she is no longer afraid. This is the attitude of a Buddha.

RIGHT PATH

Happiness means feeling you are on the right path every moment. You don't need to arrive at the end of the path in order to be happy. The right path refers to the very concrete ways you live your life in every moment. In Buddhism, we speak of the

Noble Eightfold Path: Right View, Right Thought, Right Speech, Right Action, Right Livelihood, Right Effort, Right Mindfulness, and Right Concentration. It's possible for us to live the Noble Eightfold Path every moment of our daily lives. That not only makes us happy, it makes people around us happy. If you practice the path, you become very pleasant, very fresh, and very compassionate.

Look at the tree in the front yard. The tree doesn't seem to be doing anything. It stands there, vigorous, fresh, and beautiful, and everyone profits from it. That's the miracle of being. If a tree were less than a tree, all of us would be in trouble. But if a tree is just a real tree, then there's hope and joy. That's why if you can be yourself, that is already action. Action is based on non-action; action is being.

There are people who do a lot, but who

also cause a lot of trouble. The more they try to help, the more trouble they create even if they have the best intentions. They're not peaceful, they're not happy. It's better not to try so hard but just to "be." Then peace and compassion are possible in every moment. On that foundation, everything you say or do can only be helpful. If you can make someone suffer less, if you can make them smile, you'll feel rewarded and you'll receive a lot of happiness. To feel that you're helpful, that you're useful to society: that is happiness. When you have a path and you enjoy every step on your path, you are already someone; you don't need to become someone else.

In Buddhism, we have the practice of *apranihita,* aimlessness. If you put an aim in front of you, you'll be running all your life, and happiness will never be possible. Happiness is possible only when you stop running and cherish the present moment and who you are. You don't need to be someone else; you're already a wonder of life.

3

EMOTIONS AND
RELATIONSHIPS

THE WOUNDED
CHILD INSIDE

In each of us, there is a young, suffering child. We have all had times of difficulty as children and many of us have experienced trauma. To protect and defend ourselves against future suffering, we often try to forget those painful times. Every time we're in touch with the experience of suffering, we believe we can't bear it, and we stuff our feelings and memories deep down in our unconscious mind. It may be that we haven't dared to face this child for many decades.

But just because we may have ignored the child doesn't mean she or he isn't there. The wounded child is always there, trying to get our attention. The child says, "I'm here. I'm here. You can't avoid me. You can't run away from me." We want to end our suffering by sending the child to a deep place inside, and staying as far away as possible. But running away doesn't end our suffering; it only prolongs it.

When we become aware that we've forgotten the wounded child in ourselves, we feel great compassion for that child and we begin to generate the energy of mindfulness. The practices of mindful walking, mindful sitting, and mindful breathing are our foundation. With our mindful breath and mindful steps, we can produce the energy of mindfulness and return to the awakened wisdom lying in each cell of our body. That energy will embrace us and heal us, and will heal the wounded child in us.

The first function of mindfulness is to recognize and not to fight. We can stop at any time and become aware of the child within us. When we recognize the wounded child for the first time, all we need to do is be aware of him or her and say hello. That's all. Perhaps this child is sad. If we notice this we can just breathe in and say to ourselves, "Breathing in, I know that sorrow has manifested in me. Hello, my sorrow. Breathing out, I will take good care of you."

Once we have recognized our inner child, the second function of mindfulness is to embrace him or her. This is a very pleasant practice. Instead of fighting our emotions, we are taking good care of ourselves. Mindfulness brings with her an ally—concentration. The first few minutes of recognizing and embracing our inner child with tenderness will bring some relief. The difficult emotions will still be there, but we won't suffer as much anymore.

After recognizing and embracing our inner child, the third function of mindfulness is to soothe and relieve our difficult emotions. Just by holding this child gently, we are soothing our difficult emotions and we can begin to feel at ease. When we embrace our strong emotions with mindfulness and concentration, we'll be able to see the roots of these mental formations. We'll know where our suffering has come from. When we see the roots of things, our suffering will lessen. So mindfulness recognizes, embraces, and relieves.

The energy of mindfulness contains the energy of concentration as well as the energy of insight. Concentration helps us focus on just one thing. With concentration, the energy of looking becomes more powerful and insight is possible. Insight always has the power of liberating us. If mindfulness is there, and we know how to keep mindfulness alive, concentration will be there too. And if we know how to keep concentration alive, insight will also come. The energy of mindfulness enables us to look deeply and gain the insight we need so that transformation is possible.

APPROPRIATE ATTENTION

If we were abused as a seven-year-old, we'll carry within us an image of that seven-year-old who is vulnerable and full of fear. When we hear something that reminds us of our suffering, it automatically puts us in touch with that old image. Many things that we see, hear, and experience in the present moment have the effect of bringing us back to that memory of suffering.

If we have been abused as a child, almost anything we see or hear can bring us back to that image of being abused. Being so constantly in touch with these images of the past can give rise to feelings of fear, anger, and despair. We call this "inappropriate attention" (*ayoniso manaskara*) because it takes us away from the present moment and into a place of old suffering. It's very important that whenever our attention is brought to that place, to that kind of image, we have ways of dealing with the sorrow, fear, and suffering that arise.

The sound of the meditation bell is a reminder for us to stop our thinking and talking, and go back to our in-breath and our out-breath. The sound of the bell can take us away from the image of suffering and remind us to enjoy breathing in deeply, calming our body and mind, smiling. When suffering arises, our practice is to breathe in and out and say, "Breathing in, I know that suffering is in me." Recognizing and embracing the mental formation is our practice. And if we do well, we can go further. With mindfulness and concentration, we can go back to the image and know what has made it arise: I have *this* because I have been in touch with *that*.

Many of us can't get out of the world of images. With the energy of mindfulness, we recognize that our old suffering is only an image; it's not reality. And we can see that life with all its wonders is here, that living happily in the present moment is possible, and then we can change the whole situation.

THE SECOND ARROW

We humans have lost the capacity of resting. We worry too much. We don't allow our bodies to heal. We don't allow our minds to heal. Even when we're given a few weeks of vacation, we don't know how to rest. Our worries, stress, and fear make the situation worse. Meditation can help release the tension, help us embrace our worries, our fear, our anger; and that is very healing. It's very important to learn again the art of resting and relaxing.

When we're at peace with ourselves, the elements of our body and mind will work together harmoniously, and that is the foundation of health. Different elements of the body will come together and work in harmony. The chemicals in our body will be released in the exact amount we need. We won't overproduce chemicals like adrenaline.

The Buddha speaks about the "second arrow." When an arrow strikes you, you feel pain. If a second arrow comes and strikes you in the same spot, the pain will be ten times worse. The Buddha advised that when you have some pain in your body or your mind, breathe in and out and recognize the significance of that pain but don't exaggerate its importance. If you stop to worry, to be fearful, to protest, to be angry about the pain, then you magnify the pain ten times or more. Your worry is the second arrow. You should protect yourself and not allow the second arrow to come, because the second arrow comes from you.

SEEDS

The purpose of meditation is to look at something deeply and see its roots. Whatever kind of action we take, if we look deeply into it, we'll be able to recognize the seed of that action. That seed may come from our ancestors. Whatever action we take, our ancestors are taking it at the same time with us. So father, grandfather, and great-grandfather are doing it with you; mother, grandmother, and great-grandmother are doing it with you.

Our ancestors are there in every cell of our body. There are seeds that are planted during your lifetime, but there are also seeds that were planted before you manifested as this body.

Sometimes we act without intention, but that is also action. "Habit energy" is pushing us; it pushes us to do things without our being aware. Sometimes we do something without knowing we're doing it. Even when we don't want to do something, we still do it. Sometimes we say, "I didn't want to do it, but it's stronger than me, it pushed me." So that is a seed, a habit energy, that may have come from many generations in the past.

We have inherited a lot. With mindfulness, we can become aware of the habit energy that has been passed down to us. We might see that our parents or grandparents were also very weak in ways similar to us. We can be aware without judgment that our negative habits come from these ancestral roots. We can smile at our short-comings, at our habit energy. With awareness, we have a choice; we can act another way. We can end the cycle of suffering right now.

Perhaps in the past we've noticed ourselves doing something unintentional, something we may have inherited, and we've blamed ourselves. We saw ourselves as an individual, isolated self, full of short-comings. But with awareness, we can begin to transform and let go of these habit energies. With the practice of mindfulness, we recognize that a habitual action has taken place. This is the first awareness that mindfulness brings. Then, if we're interested, mindfulness and concentration will help us look and find the roots of our action.

That action may have been inspired by something that happened yesterday, or it may be three hundred years old and have its roots in one of our ancestors. Once we become aware of our actions, we can decide whether or not something is beneficial; if it's not, we can decide not to repeat that action. If we're aware of the habit energies in us and can become more intentional in our thoughts, speech, and actions, then we can transform not only ourselves, but also our ancestors who planted the seeds. We are practicing for all our ancestors and descendants, not just for ourselves; we're practicing for the whole world.

When we're able to smile at a provocation, we can be aware of our ability, appreciate it, and continue in this way. If we're able to do that, it means our ancestors are also able to smile at what is provoking them. If one person keeps calm and smiles at a provocation, the whole world will have a better chance for peace. The key is to be aware of what our actions are.

Our mindfulness will help us understand where our actions are coming from.

BLOCKS AND KNOTS

To oppose, brush aside, or deny pain in our body or mind only makes that feeling more intense. Our painful feelings are not other than ourselves, or to put it more precisely, they are a part of us. To deny them is to deny our very selves. The moment we accept these feelings, we begin to feel more peaceful, and the pain begins to lose some of its intensity. To smile to our pain is the wisest, the most intelligent, the most beautiful thing we can do. There is no better way.

Every time we acknowledge a feeling of pain and make its acquaintance, we come in close contact with ourselves. Bit by bit we look deeply into the substance and the roots of that pain. Fear, insecurity, anger, sadness, jealousy, and attachment form blocks of feelings and thoughts within us (Sanskrit: *samyojana*, "internal formation"), and we need time and opportunity to acknowledge them and to look into them. The mindfulness of breathing does the work of making painful feelings bearable. Mindfulness recognizes the presence of the feelings, acknowledges them, soothes them, and enables the work of observation to continue until the substance of the block is seen. Mindfulness is the only way to transform it. All the seeds of pain are present within us, and if we live in forgetfulness, the seeds of pain will be watered every day. They will grow strong, and the internal blocks will become more solid. Conscious breathing transforms internal formations of painful feelings.

Internal formation can also be seen as "fetters" or "knots" of suffering deep in our consciousness. The knots are created when we react emotionally to what others say and do, and also when we repeatedly suppress our awareness of both pleasant and unpleasant feelings and thoughts. The fetters that bind us can be identified as any painful feeling or addictive pleasant feeling, such as anger, hatred, pride, doubt, sorrow, or attachment. They are forged by confusion and a lack of understanding, by our misperceptions regarding our selves and our reality. By practicing mindfulness, we are able to recognize and transform unpleasant feelings and emotions when they first arise, so they do not become fetters. When we do not let ourselves react to the words and actions of others, when we are able to keep our minds calm and peaceful, the fetters of internal formations cannot be made, and we will experience greater happiness and joy. Our families, friends, and associates will also benefit from our greater understanding and love.

WEATHERING STRONG EMOTIONS

A strong emotion is like a storm. If you look at a tree in a storm, the top of the tree seems fragile, like it might break at any moment. You are afraid the storm might uproot the tree. But if you turn your attention to the trunk of the tree, you realize that its roots are deeply anchored in the ground, and you see that the tree will be able to hold. You too are a tree. During a storm of emotion, you should not stay at the level of the head or the heart, which are like the top of the tree. You have to leave the heart, the eye of the storm, and come back to the trunk of the tree. Your trunk is one centimeter below your navel. Focus there, paying attention only to the movement of your abdomen, and continue to breathe. Then you will survive the storm of strong emotion.

It is essential to understand that an emotion is merely something that arises, remains, and then goes away. A storm comes, it stays a while, and then it moves away. At the critical moment, remember that you are much more than your emotions. This is a simple thing that everybody knows, but you may need to be reminded of it: you are much more than your emotions. Many people have no idea how to face their emotions, and they suffer because of it.

You should not wait for emotion to appear before you begin practicing. Otherwise you will be carried away by the storm. You should train now, while the emotion is not there. So sit or lie down and practice mindfulness of the breath, using the movement of your abdomen as the object of your attention. I am positive that if you do this exercise for twenty days, ten minutes per day, then you will know how to practice whenever a strong emotion comes up. After ten or twenty minutes, the emotion will go away, and you will be saved from the storm.

TAKING CARE OF
YOUR ANGER

Anger has the power to burn and destroy. If you don't know the practice of mindfulness, you will allow yourself to be burned and destroyed by anger. You will suffer and those around you will suffer as well. That is why, when you notice that anger is coming up, you have to do something right away. It is important to act, rather than react. You have to act by inviting the seed of mindfulness to arise. We breathe in and we breathe out, making steps, generating the energy of mindfulness in order to take care of our anger.

Suppose a mother is working in the living room and she hears her baby crying. Chances are she puts down whatever she is doing and goes to her baby's room. She picks up the baby and holds it tenderly in her arms. This is exactly what we can do when the energy of anger comes up. Our anger is our ailing baby. We must nurture it in order to calm it.

The practitioner knows that her anger is not her enemy; her anger is her suffering baby. She must take good care of her baby, using the energy of mindfulness to embrace her anger in the most tender way. She can say, "Breathing in, I know that anger is in me. Breathing out, I am peacefully holding my anger."

When we breathe like this, there are two kinds of energy: the energy of anger and the energy of mindfulness. The energy of mindfulness continues to be generated by the practice of mindful breathing and mindful walking, and it begins to penetrate into the zone of the angry energy. In summer, if you go into a room that is too hot, hopefully you can open a window or turn on a fan or the air conditioner.

The cool air does not need to chase the hot air out. Instead, the coolness comes and tenderly embraces the heat. And fifteen minutes later, the air is different. So it is with bringing mindfulness to our anger. There is no fighting in this practice. Your anger is not your enemy; it's you. It's not good to do violence to yourself. Don't say that mindfulness is good and anger is evil, and good has to fight evil. In this tradition of mindfulness, there is no battle to be won. Suppose we are feeling a very deep anger that will not go away. We have to be very patient. By continuing to generate the energy of mindfulness and tenderly embrace our anger, we will find relief.

MINDFULNESS OF CONSUMPTION

In order to forget that we have blocks of pain, sorrow, fear, and violence, we lose ourselves in the practice of consumption. Why do we turn on the television? Why do we continue to watch, even if the programs are not interesting at all? We watch because we want something to cover up our pain, sorrow, fear, and anger. We don't want those feelings to come up, so we suppress them by consuming.

There is some feeling of loneliness, fear, or depression inside that we don't want, so we pick up the newspaper, we turn on the radio, we turn on the television, we pick up the phone, we go for a drive. We do everything we can to avoid confronting our true selves. This kind of consumption is a practice of running away, and the items we consume continue to bring the toxins of violence, fear, and anger into us. By practicing an embargo on our negative feelings, we create a situation of bad circulation in our psyche, suppressing our unwanted thought patterns and not allowing them to circulate. When we create a situation of bad circulation in our consciousness, it causes symptoms of depression and mental illness.

When the blood in our body does not circulate well, we experience physical pain—we have a headache, a backache, sometimes there is pain everywhere. When we exercise and massage to help the blood circulate well, we diminish these symptoms in our body. The same is true with our consciousness. If we block unpleasant thought patterns through consumption, we create bad circulation in our psyche, and symptoms of mental illness will appear. That is why it's very important to lift the embargo, allowing fear, pain, and sorrow to come up.

You can only do this if you are ready, or you'll be overwhelmed by your suffering. You invite the negative thoughts to come up with the energy of mindfulness generated by your practice. This energy is there to recognize, embrace, and transform. If you practice, if you know how to sit, then the energy of mindfulness and concentration within you will be powerful enough to do the work of recognizing, embracing, and bringing relief to your suffering. After being embraced by mindfulness and finding relief, the energy of fear, anger, and depression that was growing within you will lose some of its power.

HUGGING MEDITATION

We all feel insecure. We don't know what the future holds. Accidents happen. A loved one may suddenly be struck by an incurable disease and die. We are not sure if we'll be alive tomorrow. This is all part of impermanence. This feeling of insecurity makes us suffer. How can we face this feeling? What is our practice? I think living deeply in the present moment is what we have to learn and practice to face this feeling of insecurity. We have to handle the present moment well. We live deeply in the present moment so that in the future we will have no regrets. We are aware that we and the person in front of us are both alive. We cherish the moment and do whatever we can to make life meaningful and to make him happy in this moment.

I propose hugging meditation for when

we are angry with someone in our family—and also for when we're not angry! We close our eyes, take a deep breath, and visualize ourselves and our beloved three hundred years from now. Then, the only meaningful thing to do is to open our arms and hug him. When you hug someone, first practice breathing in and breathing out to bring your insight of impermanence to life. "Breathing in, I know that life is precious in this moment. Breathing out, I cherish this moment of life." You smile at the person in front of you, expressing your desire to hold him in your arms. This is a practice and a ritual. When you bring your body and mind together to produce your total presence, to become full of life, it is a ritual.

When I drink a glass of water, I invest 100 percent of myself in drinking it. You should train yourself to live every moment of your daily life like that. Hugging is a deep practice. You need to be totally present to do it correctly. When you open your arms and hold the other person, you practice three mindful breaths. "Breathing in, I know that he is still alive in my arms. Breathing out, I feel so happy."

Life becomes real at that moment. Architects need to build airports and railway stations so that there is enough room to practice hugging. You can also practice it in the following way: during the first in-breath and out-breath, you become aware that you and your beloved are both alive; for the second in-breath and out-breath, you think of where you will both be three hundred years from now; and for the third in-breath and out-breath, you go back to the insight that you are both alive. Your hugging will be deeper, and so will your happiness.

THE ENERGY OF LOVE

We all share the fear that our need to love and be loved cannot be fulfilled. The fear of being lonely is always there, in everyone. We have to recognize that fear and that need within ourselves. The practice is to look deeply into that kind of fear. To love is to offer understanding and comfort. Understanding is the source of love. We would feel miserable if no one understood us. And when someone does not understand us, he or she cannot love us. Without understanding, love is impossible. So the truth is that we need understanding and we need love. And we are looking for someone who can provide us with both.

Suppose there is someone who is capable of offering us understanding and love. Suppose he is somewhere there, she is somewhere there. But we have to ask the question: are we capable of offering him or her understanding and love? Are we capable of generating the understanding and the love that we so need? Because if we're not capable of generating the energy of understanding, nothing will happen.

The teaching of the Buddha aims at helping us to generate the energy of love and understanding. If we can produce that energy, it will first of all help us to satisfy our need to be loved. And then, with that capacity of love and understanding, we can embrace the people who are with us now. We can make them happy while we are happy ourselves. Happiness creates more nourishment, healing, and happiness.

So the question is not "how can we obtain love and understanding?" The question is whether we have the capacity of generating love and understanding ourselves. If we do, we'll feel wonderful, because these energies satisfy us and the people around us at the same time. That is the love of the Buddha. True love is like that too. Loving one person is really an opportunity to learn to love all people. If you have the capacity to love and to understand, you can do that now, you don't have to wait. When we succeed in this, our worry and fear go away, and we feel wonderful right away.

UNDERSTANDING

Sometimes we may believe that we are acting from love, but if our action is not based in deep understanding, it will bring suffering. You want to make someone happy, and you believe very strongly that you are doing something out of love. But your action may make the other person suffer very much. So even though you believe you are acting from love, you cause your son or daughter, your partner or spouse, your friend or coworker to suffer deeply because you do not have enough understanding of that person. That is why you need the eye of understanding, of wisdom, to be an effective instrument of compassion.

If you don't understand the suffering, the difficulty, the deep aspiration of another person, it's not possible for you to love them. So it's very important to check with them and ask for help. A father should be able to ask his child, "Do I understand you well enough? Do I make you suffer because of my lack of understanding?"

A mother should be able to ask her child, "Do you think I understand you? Please tell me so that I can love you properly." That is the language of love. And if you are sincere, your daughter or son will tell you about their suffering. And when you have understood their suffering, you will stop doing things that make him or her suffer, things that you believed you did only for her happiness and well-being. Deep understanding is the substance of which true love is made. The hands of the bodhisattva symbolize action, but our actions must be guided well by the eyes of understanding.

FOUR MANTRAS

In Buddhism we talk about mantras. A mantra is a magic formula that, once it is uttered, can entirely change a situation, our mind, our body, or a person. But this magic formula must be spoken in a state of concentration, that is to say, a state in which body and mind are absolutely in a state of unity. What you say then, in this state of being, becomes a mantra.

So I am going to present to you four very effective mantras, not in Sanskrit or Tibetan, but in English.

The first mantra is "Dear one, I am here for you." Perhaps this evening you will try for a few minutes to practice mindful breathing in order to bring your body and mind together. You will approach the person you love and with this mindfulness, with this concentration, you will look into his or her eyes, and you will begin to utter this formula: "Dear one, I am really here for you." You must say that with your body and with your mind at the same time, and then you will see the transformation.

To be there is the first step, and recognizing the presence of the other is the second step. To love is to recognize; to be loved is to be recognized by the other. If you love someone and you continue to ignore his or her presence, this is not true love. Perhaps your intention is not to ignore this person, but the way you act, look, and speak does not manifest the desire to recognize the presence of the other. When we are loved, we wish the other to recognize our presence, and this is a very important practice. You must do whatever is necessary to be able to do this: recognize the presence of the person you love several times each day.

To attain this goal, it is also necessary to practice oneness of body and mind. Practice an in-breath and an out-breath three times, five times, seven times; then you approach this person, you look at him or her mindfully, with a smile, and you begin to say the second mantra: "Dear one, I know that you are here, and it makes me very happy." If you practice in this way, with a lot of concentration and mindfulness, you will see that this person will open immediately, like a flower blossoming. To be loved is to be recognized, and you can do that several times a day. It is not difficult at all, and it is a true meditation.

The third mantra is used in circumstances in which the person you love is suffering. When you are living mindfully, you know what is happening in your situation in the present moment. Therefore it is easy for you to notice when the person you love is suffering. At such a time you go to him or her, with your body and mind unified, with concentration, and you utter the third mantra: "Dear one, I know that you are suffering, that is why I am here for you." Because when we are suffering, we have a strong need for the presence of the person we love. If we are suffering and the man or woman we love ignores us, then we suffer more. So what we can do—right away—is to manifest our true presence to the beloved person and say the mantra with all our mindfulness: "Dear one, I know that you are suffering, that is why I am here for you." Even before you actually do something to help, the person you love is relieved. Your presence is a miracle, your understanding of his or her pain is a miracle, and you are able to offer this aspect of your love immediately.

The fourth mantra is more difficult to practice. It has to do with a situation in which you are suffering yourself and you think that your suffering has been created by the person you love most in the world. If it had been someone else who had said that to you or done that to you, without a doubt you would be suffering less. But in this case, it is the person I love most in the world who said that to me, who did that to me, and I am suffering more. I am deeply hurt by the fact that my suffering was caused by the person I love the most. I feel like going to my room, closing the door, staying by myself, and crying. I refuse to go to him or her to ask for help. So now it is pride that is the obstacle.

According to the teaching of the Buddha, in true love there is no place for pride. If you are suffering, every time you are suffering you must go to the person in question and ask for his or her help. That is true love. Do not let pride keep you apart. If you think your love for this person is true love, you must overcome your pride; you must always go to him or her. That is why I have invented this mantra for you. Practice so as to bring about oneness of your body and mind before going to the person to say the fourth mantra: "Dear one, I am suffering; please help."

MINDFUL COMMUNICATION

Today, communication between individuals, families, and nations has become very difficult. However, there are concrete ways to train ourselves to communicate nonviolently so that compassion for one another is awakened and mutual understanding becomes possible again.

Speaking and listening with compassion are the essential practices of nonviolent communication. Mindful communication means to be aware of what we are saying and to use conscious, loving speech. It also means listening deeply to the other person to hear what is being said and what is not being said. We can use these methods in any situation, at any time, wherever we are.

For our body to be healthy, our heart must pump a constant flow of blood. For our relationships to be healthy, we need a constant flow of mindful communication. Yet many people find it difficult to communicate effectively because they have so much frustration and anger built up inside. Even when we come to another person with sincere goodwill and the intention to listen, if we are unable to use calm, loving speech, there is no hope that the other person will hear us and understand what we are trying to say. We may intend to use calm and loving speech, but often as we start speaking, our pain, despair, and fear emerge. In spite of our best intentions, we start to blame, complain, and judge harshly. Our speech begins to reverberate with the kind of energy that turns people against us because they cannot bear to hear what we are saying. Communication breaks down. When this happens, we need to learn, or to relearn, how to communicate.

How then do we reach the point where

we are able to listen deeply to one another and to use loving speech? To do
this, we first have to practice taking care
of our own pain and anger. By practicing
mindful breathing and mindful walking,
we strengthen the energy of mindfulness
within us. We may need to practice and
train ourselves for several weeks, or even
several months, before we can overcome
our pain and use loving speech. When our
mindfulness is strong, it is much easier to
look deeply into a situation and to give rise
to understanding and compassion. With
the energy of mindfulness, we can overcome our pain and use loving speech.

The same is true about our ability to listen deeply. If we have not been able to embrace and transform our own hurt and
anger, it will be difficult to listen to another person's suffering, especially if the
other person's speech is full of negative
judgments, misperceptions, and blaming.

In our heart, we know that listening is what we should do, and no doubt we have often tried our best. Yet frequently, after a few minutes, we no longer can bear to listen to even one more word. We feel overwhelmed. Even though we have vowed that, regardless of the provocation or unjust assertions, we would stay and listen with compassion, we just cannot do it. Our good intentions evaporate because we are unable to handle the pain welling up within ourselves.

Yet if we can prevail and listen for only one hour, the other person will obtain a great deal of relief. Listening with an open heart, we are able to keep compassion alive. Then we give the other person a real chance to express his or her feelings.

Such listening requires training and practice. The practices of mindful breathing and mindful walking can help transform the seeds of anger and irritation in us and allow us to open our hearts to listen with love and compassion to the other person.

YOUR TRUE PERSON

Often, we live a life of compromise so that there's peace in the house. We buy a small peace so that we can get through the day. And if we live like that then we aren't a great person, but a cracked vase, unable to contain the rice soup. If we want to be a great Dharma instrument, then we have to be determined not to let other people trick us.

Master Linji exhorted us to be the masters of our own situation, but that doesn't mean we need to fight and suppress others, but rather we need to be the masters of ourselves. Suppose we have a friend who is quick to anger. We can think there is something wrong with him, and try to suppress his anger. We can think that because he is raising his voice we have to raise ours. Or we can be the master of ourselves in that situation, feeling real compassion for the other person's difficulties. Sometimes it's not a person in the moment but a person in the past who we think is the master of our situation. We say that we are behaving a certain way because of something our parents or someone else did to us as a child. But each person has their own karma and each person is the master of their own situation in the moment, not a slave to others past or present.

The true person doesn't go looking for an outside master. We are in charge of our own destiny and we have to be responsible for each of our words, thoughts, and actions. Mindfulness will help. Then we realize, "I'm thinking like this, I'm responsible for these thoughts. I've spoken like that, I'm responsible for my words. I'm doing this, and I'm responsible for this action." We have to know that each word, each thought, each of our actions carries our signature. We are responsible for it and that is called being in charge of ourselves. Wherever we stand, wherever we sit, we are the true person. We are masters of ourselves and wherever we are, we are ourselves. We only need to live these eight words, and it's enough to make us Master Linji's student, worthy to be his continuation: "Wherever we are, we are our true person." Write these words and hang them somewhere to remind yourself.

WRONG PERCEPTIONS

A man once had to leave home for a long time. Before he left, his wife got pregnant, but he didn't know it. When he returned, his wife had given birth to a child. He suspected that the little boy was not his, and believed that he was the son of a neighbor who used to come and work for the family. He looked at the little boy with suspicion. He hated him. He saw the neighbor's face in the little boy's face. Then once day the man's brother came to visit for the first time. When he saw the little boy, he said to the father, "He looks just like you. He's your exact duplicate." The brother's visit was a happy event, because it helped the father to get rid of his wrong perception. But the wrong perception had controlled this man's life for twelve years. It made the father suffer deeply. It made his wife suffer deeply, and, of course, the little boy suffered from that kind of hatred.

We act on the basis of wrong perceptions all the time. We should not be sure of any perception we have. When you look at the beautiful sunset, you may be quite sure that you are seeing the sun as it is in that moment, but a scientist will tell you that the image of the sun that you see is the image of the sun from eight minutes ago. Sunlight takes eight minutes to reach the earth from such a long distance. Also, when you see a star, you think that the star is there, but the star may have disappeared already, one, two, or ten thousand years before.

We have to be very careful with our perceptions, otherwise we will suffer. It is very helpful to write on a piece of paper, "Are you sure?" and hang it up in your room. In medical clinics and hospitals, they are beginning to hang up these kinds of signs: "Even if you are sure, check again." It is a caution that if a disease is not detected early, then it will be very difficult to heal. The medical doctors are not thinking in terms of mental formations. They are thinking in terms of a hidden disease. But we can also make use of this slogan— "Even if you are sure, check again." We have made ourselves suffer, we made a hell for ourselves and our beloved ones because of our perceptions. Are you sure of your perception?

There are people who suffer from a wrong perception for ten or twenty years. They are sure the other person has betrayed them or hates them, even though the other person has betrayed only good intentions. A person who is the victim of a wrong perception makes himself and the people around him suffer a lot.

When you are angry, and you suffer, please go back and inspect very deeply the content, the nature of your perceptions. If you are capable of removing the wrong perception, peace and happiness will be restored in you, and you will be able to love the other person again.

LETTING GO

To "let go" means to let go of *something*. That something may be an object of our mind, something we've created, like an idea, feeling, desire, or belief. Getting stuck on that idea could bring a lot of unhappiness and anxiety. We'd like to let it go, but how? It's not enough just to want to let it go; we have to recognize it first as being something real. We have to look deeply into its nature and where it has come from, because ideas are born from feelings, emotions, and past experiences, from things we've seen and heard. With the energy of mindfulness and concentration we can look deeply and discover the roots of the idea, the feeling, the emotion, the desire. Mindfulness and concentration bring about insight, and insight can help us release the object in our mind.

Say you have a notion of happiness, an idea about what will make you happy. That idea has its roots in you and your environment. The idea tells you what conditions you need in order to be happy. You've entertained the idea for ten or twenty years, and now you realize that your idea of happiness is making you suffer. There may be an element of delusion, anger, or craving in it. These elements are the substance of suffering. On the other hand, you know that you have other kinds of experiences: moments of joy, release, or true love. You recognize these as moments of real happiness. When you have had a moment of real happiness, it becomes easier to release the objects of your craving, because you are developing the insight that these objects will not make you happy.

Many people have the desire to let go, but they're not able to do so because they don't yet have enough insight; they haven't seen other alternatives, other doorways to peace and happiness. Fear is an element that prevents us from letting go. We're fearful that if we let go we'll have nothing else to cling to. Letting go is a practice; it's an art. One day, when you're strong enough and determined enough, you'll let go of the afflictions that make you suffer.

INFERIORITY

Many people have the idea that they are not good at anything, that they are not able to be as successful as other people. They cannot be happy; they envy the accomplishments and social standing of others while regarding themselves as failures if they do not have the same level of worldly success.

We have to try to help those who feel this way. We must come to them and say, "You should not have an inferiority complex. I see in you some very good seeds that can be developed and make you into a great being. If you look more deeply within and get in touch with those wholesome seeds in you, you will be able to overcome your feelings of unworthiness and manifest your true nature." The Chinese teacher Master Guishan writes,

We should not look down on
    ourselves.
We should not see ourselves as
    worthless and always withdraw
    into the background.

These words are designed to wake us up. In modern society, psychotherapists report that many people suffer from low self-esteem. They feel that they are worthless and have nothing to offer, and many of them sink into depression and can no longer function well or take care of themselves or their families. Therapists, healers, caregivers, teachers, religious leaders, and those who are close to someone who suffers in this way all have the duty to help them see their true nature more clearly so that they can free themselves from the delusion that they are worthless. If we know friends or family members who see themselves as worthless, powerless, and incapable of doing anything good or meaningful, and this negative self-image has taken away all their happiness, we have to try to help our friend, our sister or brother, our parent, spouse, or partner remove this complex.

We also have to practice so as not to add to others' feelings of worthlessness. In our daily life when we become impatient or irritated, we might say things that are harsh, judgmental, and critical, especially in regard to our children. When they are under a great deal of pressure, working very hard to support and care for their family, parents frequently make the mistake of uttering unkind, punitive, or blaming words in moments of stress or irritation. The ground of a child's consciousness is still very young, still very fresh, so when we sow such negative seeds in our children, we are destroying their capacity to be happy. So parents and teachers, siblings, and friends all have to be very careful and practice mindfulness in order to avoid sowing negative seeds in the minds of our children, family members, friends, and students.

HEALING THE PAST

Our presence here means the presence of all our ancestors. They are still alive in us.

Every time we smile, all the generations of our ancestors, our children, and the generations to come—all of whom are within us—smile too. We practice not just for ourselves, but for everyone, and the stream of life continues. If you have made mistakes and caused your beloved to suffer, and if he or she is no longer alive, don't be frustrated. You can still heal the wound within you. The person whom you think has passed away is still alive in you. You can make him or her smile. Suppose while your grandma was alive, you said something out of forgetfulness that made her unhappy and you still regret it. Sit down, breathe in and out mindfully, visualize your grandma sitting with you, and say, "Grandma, I am. I will never again say anything like that to you or anyone else I love." If you are sincere, focused, and utterly mindful, you will see her smiling in you and the wound will be healed.

Mistakes come from unskillfulness and forgetfulness, which are in the mind. Because everything comes from the mind, everything can be removed and transformed by the mind. That is the teaching of the Buddha.

Although we think the past is gone and the future is not yet here, if we look deeply we see that reality is more than that. The past exists in the guise of the present because the present is made from the past. In this teaching, if we establish ourselves firmly in the present and touch the present moment deeply, we also touch the past and have the power to repair it. That is a wonderful teaching and practice. We don't have to bear our wounds forever. We are all unmindful at times; we have made mistakes in the past. It does not mean that we have to always carry that guilt without transforming it. Touch the present deeply and you touch the past. Take care of the present and you can repair the past. The practice of beginning anew is a practice of the mind. Once you realize what mistake you made in the past, you are determined never to do it again. Then the wound is healed. It is a wonderful practice.

WALKING WITH YOUR PARENTS

When you walk, for whom do you walk? You can walk to get somewhere, but you can also walk as a kind of meditative offering. It's very nice to walk for your parents or for your grandparents who may not have known the practice of walking in mindfulness. Your ancestors may have spent their whole life without the chance to make peaceful, happy steps and establish themselves fully in the present moment. This is a great pity, but we do not need to repeat this situation.

All our ancestors and all future generations are present in us. Liberation is not an individual matter. As long as the ancestors in us are still suffering, we cannot be happy, and we will transmit that suffering to our children and their children.

Now is the time to liberate our ancestors and future generations: to free ourselves. If we can take one step freely and happily, touching the earth mindfully, we can take one hundred. We do it for ourselves and for all previous and future generations. We all arrive at the same time and find peace and happiness together!

When you make a step, you may visualize that your mother is taking that step with you. This is not something difficult, because you know that your feet are a continuation of the feet of your mother. As we practice looking deeply, we see the presence of our mother in every cell of our body. Our body is also a continuation of our mother's body. When you make a step, you may say, "Mother, walk with me." And suddenly you feel your mother in you walking with you. You may notice that during her lifetime she did not have much chance to walk in the here and the now and to enjoy touching the earth like you. Suddenly compassion, love, is born. And that is because you can see your mother walking with you—not as something imagined but as a reality.

You can invite your father to walk with you. You may like to invite the people you love to walk with you in the here and the now. You can invite them and walk with them without the need for them to be physically present. We continue our ancestors; our ancestors are fully present in every cell of our body. When we take a peaceful step we know that all of our ancestors are taking that step with us. Millions of feet are making the same movement. With video techniques you can create that kind of image. Thousands of feet are making a step together. And of course your mind can do that. Your mind can see thousands and millions of your ancestors' feet are making a step together with you. That practice, using visualization, will shatter the idea, the feeling, that you are a separate self. You walk, and yet they walk.

It is possible for you to walk with the feet of your mother. Poor mother, she didn't have much opportunity to walk like this. You can say, "Mother, would you like to walk with me?" And then you walk with her, and your heart will fill with love. You free yourself and you free her at the same time, because it's true that your mother is in you, in every cell of your body. Your father is also fully present in every cell of your body. You can say, "Dad, would you like to join me?" Then suddenly you walk with the feet of your father. It's a joy. It's very rewarding. And I assure you that it's not difficult. You don't have to fight and struggle in order to do it. Just become aware, and everything will go well.

You may also like to sit for your mother. Many mothers don't get many opportunities to sit down and do nothing. This is important work! You can sit and just breathe mindfully, and this will be something you can do for your mother, whether she has passed on or is still with you, whether she is far away or near. After you have been able to walk for your dear ones, you can walk for the people who have made your life miserable. You can walk for those who have attacked you, who have destroyed your home, your country, and your people. These people weren't happy. They didn't have enough love for themselves and for other people. They have made your life miserable and the life of your family and your people miserable. And there will be a time when you'll be able to walk for them too. Walking like that, you become a Buddha; you become a bodhisattva filled with love, understanding, and compassion.

4

PEACE

THE SPIRITUAL
DIMENSION OF POLITICS

Every bit of our understanding, compassion, and peace is useful; it is gold. There are many things we can do today to increase these capacities in ourselves. When you take a step, if you can enjoy that step, if your step can bring you more stability and freedom, then you are serving the world. It is with that kind of peace and stability that you can serve. If you don't have the qualities of stability, peace, and freedom inside of you, then no matter what you do, you cannot help the world. It is not about "doing" something; it's about "being" something—being peace, being hope, being solid. Every action will come out of that, because peace, stability, and freedom always seek a way to express themselves in action. That is the spiritual dimension of our reality.

The basic issue is our practice of peace, our practice of looking deeply. First of all, we need to allow ourselves to calm down. Without tranquility and serenity, our emotions, anger, and despair will not go away, and we will not be able to look and see the nature of reality. Calming down, becoming serene, is the first step of meditation.

The second step is to look deeply to understand. Out of understanding comes compassion. And from this foundation of understanding and compassion, you will be able to see what you can do and what you should refrain from doing. This is meditation. Every one of us has to practice meditation—the politicians, the military, the businessmen. All of us have to practice calming down and looking deeply. You have the support of all of us in doing this.

SEEDS OF VIOLENCE

Violence is never far. It is possible to identify the seeds of violence in our everyday thoughts, speech, and actions. We can find these seeds in our own minds, in our attitudes, and in our fears and anxieties about ourselves and others. Thinking itself can be violent, and violent thoughts can lead us to speak and act violently. In this way, the violence in our minds manifests in the world.

The daily wars that occur within our thoughts and within our families have everything to do with the wars fought between peoples and nations throughout the world. The conviction that we know the truth and that those who do not share our beliefs are wrong has caused a lot of harm. When we believe something to be the absolute truth, we have become caught in our own views. If we believe, for instance, that Buddhism is the only way to happiness, we may be practicing a kind of violence by discriminating against and excluding those who follow other spiritual paths. When we are caught in our views, we are not seeing and understanding in accord with reality. Being caught in our views can be very dangerous and block the opportunity for us to gain a deeper wisdom.

We usually think of violence and war as an act or event with a definite beginning and a definite end. But when we look into the true nature of war, we see that, whether war breaks out or not, the seeds of war are already here. We do not have to wait until war is officially declared to recognize its presence. When the opposing armies have left the battlefield and gone home, it seems that war no longer exists, but that may not really be true. The war may still be there. Although the fighting has ended, hatred and fear are still there in the hearts and minds of the soldiers and the soldiers' fellow citizens. The war is there, yes, and if we look around we will recognize its many faces: religious intolerance, ethnic hatred, child neglect, racial discrimination, and exploitation of the world's resources. But we also know that the seeds of peace, understanding, and love are there and that they will grow if we cultivate them.

When we recognize the violence that has taken root within us, in the everyday way we think, speak, and act, we can wake up and live in a new way. We can make a strong determination to live mindfully, to live in peace. Shining the light of awareness on the roots of violence within our own hearts and thoughts, we can stop the war where it begins, in our minds. Stopping the war in our minds and in our hearts, we will surely know how to stop the war outside.

ENGAGED BUDDHISM

In Vietnam we started a movement that we called "Engaged Buddhism." We wanted Buddhism to be present in every walk of life—not just in the temple, but also in society, in our schools, our families, and our workplaces, even in politics and the military. Compassion and understanding should be present everywhere.

There are many of us who are eager to work for peace, but we don't have peace within. Angrily we shout for peace. And angrily we shout at the people who, like us, are also for peace; even people and groups dedicated to peacemaking sometimes fight among themselves. If there is no peace in our hearts, there can be no harmony among the peace workers. And if there is no harmony, there is no hope. If we're divided, if we're in despair, we can't serve; we can't do anything. Peace must begin with ourselves: with the practice of sitting quietly, walking mindfully, taking care of our body, releasing the tension in our body and in our feelings. That is why the practice of being peace is at the foundation of the practice of doing peace. Being peace comes first. Doing peace is something that comes from that foundation.

The moment when you sit down and begin to breathe in, calming your mind and your body, peace has become a reality. That kind of breathing is like praying. When there is the element of peace in you, you can connect with other people, and you can help others to be peaceful like you. Together you become a body of peace, the Sangha body of peace. The practice can bring peace to us right away; and when you're more peaceful, more pleasant, you can be more effective in contacting other people and inviting them to join in the work of peacemaking. Since you're peaceful and you know how to look peacefully, speak peacefully, and react peacefully, you can persuade many people to join you in the work of promoting peace and reconciliation.

You can't have peace just by sitting down and negotiating or making plans. You have to learn to breathe in and out, to calm yourself, and you have to be able to help the other person to do like you. If there's no element of peace in you and in the other person, none of your activities can be described as genuine acts of peacemaking.

We have to practice peace in our corporations, our cities, and our schools. Schoolteachers have to practice peace, and teach their students how to practice peace.

The president of a country or the head of a political party must practice peace, must pray for peace in his body and mind before he can be effective in asking other prime ministers and heads of state to join him in making peace. Ideally each peace conference would begin with walking meditation and sitting meditation. And someone would be there to guide the total relaxation in order to remove tension, anger, and fear in body and mind. That is bringing the spiritual dimension into our political and social life; that is Engaged Buddhism.

HEROISM

Understanding and compassion are very powerful sources of energy. They are the opposite of stupidity and passivity. If you think that compassion is passive, weak, or cowardly, then you don't know what real understanding or compassion is. If you think that compassionate people do not resist and challenge injustice, you are wrong. They are warriors, heroes, and heroines who have gained many victories. When you act with compassion, with nonviolence, when you act on the basis of nonduality, you have to be very strong. You no longer act out of anger; you do not punish or blame. Compassion grows constantly inside of you, and you can succeed in your fight against injustice. Mahatma Gandhi was just one person. He did not have any bombs, any guns, or any political party. He acted simply on the insight of nonduality, the strength of compassion, not on the basis of anger.

Human beings are not our enemy. Our enemy is not the other person. Our enemy is the violence, ignorance, and injustice in us and in the other person. When we are armed with compassion and understanding, we fight not against other people, but against the tendency to invade, to dominate, and to exploit. We don't want to kill others, but we will not let them dominate and exploit us or other people. You have to protect yourself. You are not stupid. You are very intelligent and you have insight. Being compassionate does not mean allowing other people to do violence to themselves or to you. Being compassionate means being intelligent. Nonviolent action that springs from love can only be intelligent action.

THE THOUSAND ARMS OF THE BODHISATTVA

In many Asian Buddhist temples, there is a statue of Avalokiteshvara Bodhisattva with a thousand arms. Each arm holds an instrument or object that represents a different sphere of activity in which the bodhisattva can manifest compassion and understanding. In one hand he holds a book—it might be a sutra text or a book on political science. Another hand holds a ritual instrument, such as a bell. Another holds a musical instrument. A modern version of the thousand-armed bodhisattva might hold a computer in one hand.

Perhaps the bodhisattva holds a gun in one of its thousand hands. Is it possible to carry a weapon and yet remain deeply a bodhisattva? This is possible. At the gates of temples in Vietnam, you often see two figures: on the left is a statue of a very gentle bodhisattva, smiling, welcoming, while on the right is a figure with a very fierce expression, brandishing a weapon. In Vietnamese the name of this figure means literally "burning-face bodhisattva"—his face is burning, his eyes are burning, fire and smoke are coming out of his nose and mouth. This is the archetype of the fierce, guardian bodhisattva, one who has the capacity to keep the hungry ghosts in check. When we offer ceremonial food and drink to the hungry ghosts, we evoke this bodhisattva to come and help, because the hungry ghosts bring so much noise and disorder with them. We need the burning-face bodhisattva; we need his ferocity to help establish order, because only he can tame the wild hungry ghosts. He is a kind of police chief bodhisattva.

Yet this fierce-looking character is a manifestation of Avalokiteshvara, who takes various forms—as a gentle, motherly bodhisattva, or as a fierce guardian bodhisattva, even as a hungry ghost—in order to better understand and communicate with those he or she has come to help. Some of these manifestations may not look to us like our usual idea of a bodhisattva. If we look for Avalokiteshvara only in a nice, gentle appearance, we may miss him. We have to look deeply in order to recognize the bodhisattva of compassion in his or her many forms. If you look closely at the figure of the thousand-armed bodhisattva, you will see that in the palm of each hand there is an eye. The eye symbolizes the presence of understanding and wisdom, *prajña*. We need both compassion and wisdom to progress on the path. Understanding and wisdom help to bring about love, kindness, and compassion. Avalokiteshvara has so many arms because love needs to express itself in many different forms and through the use of many kinds of instruments. That is why every arm is holding a different instrument, and in every hand there is the eye of wisdom.

THE PEACEFUL
REVOLUTION

Some people spend their whole life trying only to get revenge. This kind of desire or volition will bring great suffering not only to others but to oneself as well. Hatred is a fire that burns in every soul and can only be tempered by compassion. But where do we find compassion? It isn't sold in the supermarket. If it were, we would only need to bring it home and we could solve all the hatred and violence in the world very easily. But compassion can only be produced in our own heart by our own practice.

Right now America is burning with fear, suffering, and hatred. If only to ease our suffering, we have to return to ourselves and seek to understand why we are caught up in so much violence. What has caused terrorists to hate so much that they are willing to sacrifice their own lives and create so much suffering for other people? We see their great hatred, but what lies underneath it? Injustice. Of course we have to find a way to stop their violence; we may even need to keep people locked in prison while their hatred burns. But the important thing is to look deeply and ask, "What responsibility do we have for the injustice in the world?"

Sometimes someone we love—our child, our spouse, or our parent—says or does something cruel and we suffer and get angry. We think it is only we who suffer. But the other person is suffering as well. If he wasn't suffering, he wouldn't have spoken or acted out of anger. The person we love doesn't know a way out of his suffering.

This is why our beloved pours out all his hatred and violence on to us. Our responsibility is to produce the energy of compassion that calms down our own heart and allows us to help the other person. If we punish the other person, he will just suffer more. Responding to violence with violence can only bring more violence, more injustice, and more suffering, not only to others but also to ourselves. This wisdom is in every one of us. When we breathe deeply, we can touch this seed of wisdom in us. I know that if the energy of wisdom and of compassion in the American people could be nourished for even one week, it would reduce the level of anger and hatred in the country. I urge all of us to practice calming and concentrating our minds, watering the seeds of wisdom and compassion that are already in us, and learning the art of mindful consumption. If we can do this, we will create a true peaceful revolution, the only kind of revolution that can help us get out of this difficult situation.

LABELS

We are separated by labels, by words like "Israeli," "Palestinian," "Buddhist," "Jew," and "Muslim." When we hear one of these words, it evokes an image and we immediately feel alienated from the other group or person. We've set up many habitual ways of thinking that separate us from each other, and we make each other suffer. So it's important to discover the human being in the other person, and to help the other person discover the human being in us. As human beings we're exactly the same. But the many layers of labels prevent other people from seeing you as a human being. Thinking of yourself as or calling yourself a "Buddhist" can be a disadvantage, because if you wear the title "Buddhist," that may be an obstacle which prevents others from discovering the human being in you. The same is true whether you are Christian, Jewish, or Muslim. This can be an important part of your identity, but it is not the whole of who you are. People are caught in these notions and images, and they cannot recognize each other as human beings. The practice of peeling away all the labels so that the human being can be revealed is truly a practice for peace. Because people are very attached to these names and labels, it is important that we use gentle language and loving speech as we talk with people about matters of identity and injustice.

Injustice is suffered by both sides in any personal dispute. It's crucial we understand that. Once understanding and compassion are born in our heart, the poisons of anger, violence, hatred, and despair will be transformed. The path is quite clear. The only solution is to get the poisons out and to get the insight and the compassion in! Then we will discover each other as human beings, not allowing ourselves to be deceived by the outer layers, by names like "Buddhism," "Islam," "Judaism," "pro-American," "pro-Arab," and so on. This is a process of liberation—liberation from our ideas, our ignorance, our tendency to discriminate. The Earth is so beautiful and there is room enough for all of us, yet we kill each other. But when we can see each other as human beings with their own suffering, we won't have the courage to shoot each other. We'll work together for the chance to live peacefully together.

INCLUSIVENESS

Each of us must ask ourselves: how large is my heart? How can I help my heart grow bigger and bigger every day? The practice of inclusiveness is based on the practice of understanding, compassion, and love.

When you practice looking deeply to understand suffering, the nectar of compassion will arise naturally in your heart. *Maitri,* loving-kindness, and *karuna,* compassion, can continue to grow indefinitely. So thanks to the practice of looking deeply and understanding, your loving-kindness and compassion grow day by day. And with enough understanding and love you can embrace and accept everything and everyone.

Very often in a conflict we feel that if those on the other side, those who oppose us or believe differently from us, ceased to exist then we would have peace and happiness. So we may be motivated by the desire to annihilate, to destroy the other side, to remove certain people from our community or society. But looking deeply we will see that just as we have suffered, they have also suffered. If we truly want to live in peace, safety, and security, we must create an opportunity for those on the other side to live this way as well. If we know how to allow the other side into our heart, if we have that intention, we not only suffer less right away but we also increase our own chances of having peace and security. When we're motivated by the intention to practice inclusiveness, it becomes very easy to ask, "How can we best help you so that you can enjoy safety? Please tell us." We express our concern for their safety, their need to live in peace, to rebuild their country, to strengthen their society. When you are able to approach a situation of conflict in this way, it can help transform the situation very quickly. The basis for this transformation, the first thing that must happen, is the change within your own heart. You open your heart to include the other side; you want to give them the opportunity to live in peace, as you wish to live.

Societies and nations that are locked in conflict need to learn the practice of inclusiveness if they really want to find a way to live together in peace. Can our side accept the fact that the other side also needs a place to live and needs the safety and stability that can guarantee a peaceful and prosperous society? When we look deeply into the situation of those on the other side, we see that they are just like us— they also want only to have a place where they can live in safety and peace. Understanding our own suffering and our own hopes can lead to understanding the suffering and hopes of the other group. We know that if the other side does not have peace and safety, then it will not be possible for us to have peace and safety. That is the nature of interbeing. With this insight we'll be able to open our heart and embrace the other side.

RECONCILIATION

Peace and compassion go hand in hand with understanding and non-discrimination. We choose one thing over another when we discriminate. With the eyes of compassion, we can look at all of living reality at once. A compassionate person sees himself or herself in every being. With the ability to view reality from many viewpoints, we can overcome all viewpoints and act compassionately in each situation. This is the highest meaning of the word "reconciliation."

Reconciliation does not mean to sign an agreement with duplicity and cruelty. Reconciliation opposes all forms of ambition, without taking sides. Most of us want to take sides in each encounter or conflict. We distinguish right from wrong based on partial evidence gathered directly or by

propaganda or hearsay. We need indignation in order to act, but indignation alone
is not enough, even righteous, legitimate
indignation. Our world does not lack people willing to throw themselves into action. What we need are people who are
capable of loving, of not taking sides so
that they can embrace the whole of reality
as a mother hen embraces all her chicks,
with two fully spread wings.

The practice of meditation on interdependent co-arising is one way to arrive at
this realization. When it is attained, discrimination vanishes and reality is no longer sliced by the sword of conceptualization.
The boundaries between good and evil are
obliterated, and means and ends are recognized as the same. We have to continue
practicing until we can see a child's body
of skin and bones in Uganda or Ethiopia as
our own, until the hunger and pain in the
bodies of all living species are our own.

Then we will have realized non-discrimination, real love.

CHILDREN OF THE EARTH

We are all children of the earth, and, at some time, she will take us back to herself again. We are continually arising from Mother Earth, being nurtured by her, and then returning to her. All life is impermanent. Like us, plants are born, live for a period of time, and then return to the earth. When they decompose, they fertilize our gardens. Living vegetables and decomposing vegetables are part of the same reality. Without one, the other cannot be. After six months, compost becomes fresh vegetables again. Plants and the earth rely on each other. Whether the earth is fresh, beautiful, and green, or whether it is arid and parched, depends on the plants. It also depends on us.

So many beings in the universe love us unconditionally. A bird's song can express joy, beauty, and purity, and evoke in us vitality and love. The trees, the water, and the air don't ask anything of us; they just love us. Even though we need this kind of love, we continue to destroy these things. We should try our best to do the least harm to all living creatures. When we garden, for example, we can learn how to grow certain plants next to our vegetables and flowers that will ward off harmful insects, deer, and rabbits without hurting them. We can use organic repellents instead of chemical pesticides in order to protect birds and honeybees. We can always strive to reduce the harm we cause to other creatures. By destroying the animals, the air, and the trees, we are destroying ourselves.

We must learn to practice unconditional love for all beings so that the animals, the air, the trees, and the minerals can continue to be themselves.

An oak tree is an oak tree. All it needs to do is to be itself. If an oak tree is less than an oak tree, we will all be in trouble. In our former lives we were rocks, clouds, and trees. We have also been an oak tree. This is not just Buddhist; it is scientific. We humans are a young species. We were plants, we were trees, and now we have become humans. We have to remember our past existences and be humble. We can learn a lot from an oak tree.

Our ecology should be a deep ecology and not only deep, but universal. There is pollution in our consciousness. Television, movies, and magazines can be ways of learning or they can be forms of pollution. They can sow seeds of violence and anxiety in us and pollute our consciousness. These things destroy us in the same way that we destroy our environment by farming with chemicals, clear-cutting trees, and polluting the water. We need to protect the ecological integrity of the earth and an ecology of the mind, or this kind of violence and recklessness will spill over into even more areas of life.

We humans think we're intelligent, but an orchid, for example, knows how to produce symmetrical flowers; a snail knows how to make a beautiful, well-proportioned shell. Compared with their knowledge, ours is not worth much at all. We should bow deeply before the orchid and the snail and join our palms reverently before the butterfly and the magnolia tree. The feeling of respect for all species will help us to recognize and cultivate the noblest nature in ourselves.

ART

By living your life, by producing works of art, you contribute to the work of the collective awakening of our people. A bodhisattva is someone who is awake, mindful, and motivated by a desire to help others to wake up. The artist, the actor, the filmmaker, the novelist may be inspired by a desire to become a bodhisattva, helping with the awakening of the people, helping them to touch the seed of joy, of peace, of happiness in themselves, helping them to remove and transform the seeds of discrimination and fear and craving. The artist can do all this. If you are motivated by that desire, you will have so much joy and energy that fame and power will not appeal to you anymore. Nothing can be compared with that kind of joy, knowing that your life on earth is beautiful and is helpful.

One day in New York City I met a Buddhist scholar and I told her about my practice of mindfulness in the vegetable garden. I enjoy growing lettuce, tomatoes, and other vegetables and I like to spend time gardening every day. She said, "You shouldn't spend your time growing vegetables. You should spend more time writing poems. Your poems are so beautiful. Everyone can grow lettuce, but not everyone can write poems like you do." I told her, "If I don't grow lettuce, I can't write poems."

When I'm taking care of the lettuce or watering my garden I don't think of poetry or writing. I focus my mind entirely on taking care of the lettuce, watering the vegetables, and so on. I enjoy every moment and I do it in a mode of "non-thinking." It's very helpful to stop the thinking. Your art is conceived in the depths of your consciousness while you're not thinking about it.

The moment when you express it is only a moment of birth, the moment you deliver the baby. For me, there must be moments when you allow the child inside you to grow, so you can do your best and your masterpiece can contain insight, understanding, and compassion.

A work of art can help people understand the nature of their suffering and have insight into how to transform the negative and to develop the positive in themselves. Writing, making a film, creating a work of art can be an act of love. That act of love nourishes you and nourishes others. If you're happy, if you know how to live deeply every moment of your life, then deep understanding, joy, and compassion can come. Your art will reflect this understanding and will share it with others.

PEACE WORK

Life is filled with suffering, but it is also filled with many wonders, such as the blue sky, the sunshine, and the eyes of a baby. To suffer is not enough. We must also be in touch with the wonders of life. They are within us and all around us, everywhere, anytime.

If we are not happy, if we are not peaceful, we can't share peace and happiness with others, even those we love, those who live under the same roof. If we are peaceful, if we are happy, we can smile and blossom like a flower, and everyone in our family, our entire society, will benefit from our peace. Do we need to make a special effort to enjoy the beauty of the blue sky? Do we have to practice to be able to enjoy it? No, we just enjoy it. Each second, each minute of our lives can be like this. Wherever we are, anytime, we have the capacity to enjoy the sunshine, the presence of each other, even the sensation of our breathing. We don't need to go to China to enjoy the blue sky. We don't have to travel into the future to enjoy our breathing. We can be in touch with these things right now. It would be a pity if we were only aware of suffering.

We are so busy we hardly have time to look at the people we love, even in our own household, and to look at ourselves. Society is organized in a way that even when we have some leisure time, we don't know how to use it to get back in touch with ourselves.

We have millions of ways to lose this precious time—we turn on the TV, or pick up the telephone, or start the car and go somewhere. We are not used to being with ourselves, and we act as if we don't like ourselves and are trying to escape from ourselves.

Meditation is to be aware of what is going on—in our bodies, in our feelings, in our minds, and in the world. Each day many thousands of children die of hunger. The superpowers have enough nuclear warheads to destroy our planet many times. Yet the sunrise is beautiful, and the rose that bloomed this morning along the wall is a miracle. Life is both dreadful and wonderful. To practice meditation is to be in touch with both aspects. Please do not think we must be solemn in order to meditate.

In fact, to meditate well, we have to smile a lot. Recently I was sitting with a group of children, and a boy named Tim was smiling beautifully. I said, "Tim, you have a very beautiful smile," and he said, "Thank you." I told him, "You don't have to thank me, I have to thank you. Because of your smile, you make life more beautiful. Instead of saying, 'Thank you,' you could say, 'You're welcome.'"

If a child smiles, if an adult smiles, that is very important. If in our daily life we can smile, if we can be peaceful and happy, not only we, but everyone will profit from it. This is the most basic kind of peace work. When I see Tim smiling, I am so happy. If he is aware that he is making other people happy, he can say, "You're welcome."

THE FIVE MINDFULNESS TRAININGS

The Five Mindfulness Trainings represent the Buddhist vision for a global spirituality and ethic. They are a concrete expression of the Buddha's teachings on the Four Noble Truths and the Noble Eightfold

Path, the path of right understanding and true love, leading to healing, transformation, and happiness for ourselves and for the world. To practice the Five Mindfulness Trainings is to cultivate the insight of interbeing, or Right View, which can remove all discrimination, intolerance, anger, fear, and despair. If we live according to the Five Mindfulness Trainings, we are already on the path of a bodhisattva. Knowing we are on that path, we are not lost in confusion about our life in the present or in fears about the future.

1. *Reverence for Life*

Aware of the suffering caused by the destruction of life, I am committed to cultivating the insight of interbeing and compassion and learning ways to protect the lives of people, animals, plants, and minerals. I am determined not to kill, not to let others kill, and not to support any act of killing in the world, in my thinking, or in my way of life. Seeing that harmful actions arise from anger, fear, greed, and intolerance, which in turn come from dualistic and discriminative thinking, I will cultivate openness, non-discrimination, and non-attachment to views in order to transform violence, fanaticism, and dogmatism in myself and in the world.

2. *True Happiness*

Aware of the suffering caused by exploitation, social injustice, stealing, and oppression, I am committed to practicing generosity in my thinking, speaking, and acting. I am determined not to steal and not to possess anything that should belong to others; and I will share my time, energy, and material resources with those who are in need. I will practice looking deeply to see that the happiness and suffering of others are not separate from my own happiness and suffering; that true happiness is not possible without understanding and compassion; and that running after wealth, fame, power, and sensual pleasures can bring much suffering and despair. I am aware that happiness depends on my mental attitude and not on external conditions, and that I can live happily in the present moment simply by remembering that I already have more than enough conditions to be happy. I am committed to practicing Right Livelihood so that I can help reduce the suffering of living beings on earth and reverse the process of global warming.

3. *True Love*

Aware of the suffering caused by sexual misconduct, I am committed to cultivating responsibility and learning ways to protect the safety and integrity of individuals, couples, families, and society. Knowing that sexual desire is not love, and that sexual activity motivated by craving always harms myself as well as others, I am determined not to engage in sexual relations without true love and a deep, long-term commitment made known to my family and friends. I will do everything in my power to protect children from sexual abuse and to prevent couples and families from being broken by sexual misconduct. Seeing that body and mind are one, I am committed to learning appropriate ways to take care of my sexual energy and cultivating loving-kindness, compassion, joy, and inclusiveness—which are the four basic elements of true love—for my greater happiness and the greater happiness of others. Practicing true love, we know that we will continue beautifully into the future.

4. *Loving Speech and Deep Listening*

Aware of the suffering caused by unmindful speech and the inability to listen to others, I am committed to cultivating loving speech and compassionate listening in order to relieve suffering and to promote reconciliation and peace in myself and among other people, ethnic and religious groups, and nations. Knowing that words can create happiness or suffering, I am committed to speaking truthfully using words that inspire confidence, joy, and hope. When anger is manifesting in me, I am determined not to speak. I will practice mindful breathing and walking in order to recognize and to look deeply into my anger. I know that the roots of anger can be found in my wrong perceptions and lack of understanding of the suffering in myself and in the other person. I will speak and listen in a way that can help myself and the other person to transform suffering and see the way out of difficult situations. I am determined not to spread news that I do not know to be certain and not to utter words that can cause division or discord. I will practice Right Diligence to nourish my capacity for understanding, love, joy, and inclusiveness, and gradually transform anger, violence, and fear that lie deep in my consciousness.

5. Nourishment and Healing

Aware of the suffering caused by unmindful consumption, I am committed to cultivating good health, both physical and mental, for myself, my family, and my society by practicing mindful eating, drinking, and consuming. I will practice looking deeply into how I consume the Four Kinds of Nutriments, namely edible foods, sense impressions, volition, and consciousness. I am determined not to gamble, nor to use alcohol, drugs, or any other products that contain toxins, such as certain websites, electronic games, TV programs, films, magazines, books, and conversations. I will practice coming back to the present moment to be in touch with the refreshing, healing, and nourishing elements in me and around me, not letting regrets and sorrow drag me back into the past nor letting anxieties, fear, or craving pull me out of the present moment. I am determined not to try to cover up loneliness, anxiety, or other suffering by losing myself in consumption. I will contemplate interbeing and consume in a way that preserves peace, joy, and well-being in my body and consciousness, and in the collective body and consciousness of my family, my society, and the Earth.

SOURCES

A Life of Miracles: *The Sun My Heart*, pp. 39–41

Your True Home: *A Rose for Your Pocket*, pp. 24–27

Concentration: *You Are Here*, pp. 77–78

Freedom: *Keeping the Peace*, pp. 8–9

Resting: *Shambhala Sun*, March 1998

Loving Presence: *You Are Here*, pp. 8–10

Mindfulness of Breath: *You Are Here*, pp. 5–8

Walk like a Buddha: *Buddha Mind, Buddha Body*, pp. 1–4

Touching the Earth: *A Rose for Your Pocket*, pp. 52–53

Mindful Living: *Keeping the Peace*, pp. 17–18

Ruling the Five Skandhas: *Love's Garden*, pp. xv–xvii

Habit Energy: *The Heart of the Buddha's Teaching*, pp. 24–25

Darkness Becomes Light: *The Sun My Heart*, pp. 12–13

A Day of Mindfulness: *The Miracle of Mindfulness*, pp. 27–31

Interbeing: *The Heart of Understanding*, pp. 3–5

The Buddha: *The Heart of the Buddha's Teaching*, pp. 3–5

Impermanence: *The Heart of the Buddha's Teaching*, pp. 131–133

Deep Seeing: *Our Appointment with Life*, pp. 44–46

Nothing to Attain: *The Heart of the Buddha's Teaching*, pp. 152–53

Beyond Birth and Death: *You Are Here*, pp. 85–88

Pure Land: *Buddha Mind, Buddha Body*, pp. 64–65

The Two Dimensions: *Peaceful Action, Open Heart*, pp. 31–33

Hide and Seek: *Peaceful Action, Open Heart*, pp. 110–111

No Fear: *Answers from the Heart*, pp. 77–78

The Zen Master: *Zen Keys*, pp. 54–55

Three Doors of Liberation: *Understanding Our Mind*, pp. 242–243

The Businessless Person: *Nothing to Do, Nowhere to Go*, pp. 10–13

SOURCES

Smile of the Bodhisattva: *Understanding Our Mind*, pp. 245–246

Right Path: *Answers from the Heart*, pp. 16–17

The Wounded Child Inside: *Reconciliation*, pp. 1–3, 14–15

Appropriate Attention: *Reconciliation*, pp. 30–31

The Second Arrow: *Answers from the Heart*, pp. 127–129

Seeds: *Reconciliation*, pp. 24–26

Blocks and Knots: *The Blooming of a Lotus*, pp. 76–78

Weathering Strong Emotions: *You Are Here*, pp. 72–73

Taking Care of Your Anger: *Keeping the Peace*, pp. 24–26

Mindfulness of Consumption: *Keeping the Peace*, pp. 24–26

Hugging Meditation: *A Rose for Your Pocket*, pp. 59–61

The Energy of Love: *Answers from the Heart*, pp. 53–55

Understanding: *Peaceful Action, Open Heart*, pp. 180–181, 184–185

Four Mantras: *True Love*, pp. 9–25

Mindful Communication: *Creating True Peace*, pp. 20–22

Your True Person: *Nothing to Do, Nowhere to Go*, p. 128

Wrong Perceptions: *Anger*, pp. 78–80

Letting Go: *Answers from the Heart*, pp. 23–24

Inferiority: *Peaceful Action, Open Heart*, pp. 102–104

Healing the Past: *A Rose for Your Pocket*, pp. 43–45

Walking with Your Parents: *A Rose for Your Pocket*, pp. 47–51

The Spiritual Dimension of Politics: *Calming the Fearful Mind*, pp. 40–41

Seeds of Violence: *Creating True Peace*, pp. 11–12

Engaged Buddhism: *Answers from the Heart*, pp. 95–97

Heroism: *Anger*, pp. 128–29

The Thousand Arms of the Bodhisattva: *Peaceful Action, Open Heart*, pp. 180–181, 184–185

The Peaceful Revolution: *Calming the Fearful Mind*, pp. 58–59

Labels: *Answers from the Heart*, pp. 122–124

Inclusiveness: *Peaceful Action, Open Heart*, pp. 256–257

Reconciliation: *The Sun My Heart*, pp. 128–129

Children of the Earth: *The World We Have*, pp. 83–85

Art: *Answers from the Heart*, pp. 113–114

Peace Work: *Being Peace*, pp. 13–14.

CREDITS

Nhat Hanh. Published by Doubleday & Company, a division of Random House, Inc.

LIBRARY OF CONGRESS
CATALOGING-IN-PUBLICATION DATA

Nhât Hạnh, Thích
[Works. Selections. 2012]
The pocket Thich Nhat Hanh / compiled and edited by Melvin
McLeod.—First Edition.
pages cm
ISBN 978-1-59030-936-0 (pbk.)
1. Religious life—Buddhism.
I. Mcleod, Melvin, editor of compilation. II. Title.
BQ9800.T5392N452 2012
294.3′927—dc23
2012005545

SHAMBHALA POCKET CLASSICS

THE ART OF PEACE:
Teachings of the Founder of Aikido
by Morihei Ueshiba
Compiled and translated by John Stevens

THE ART OF WAR by Sun Tzu
Translated by Thomas Cleary

AWAKENING LOVING-KINDNESS
by Pema Chödrön

DHAMMAPADA:
The Sayings of the Buddha
Rendered by Thomas Byrom

HAGAKURE: The Book of the Samurai
by Yamamoto Tsunetomo
Translated by William Scott Wilson

I CHING:
The Book of Change
Translated by Thomas Cleary

THE MAN WHO PLANTED TREES
by Jean Giono

(Continued on next page)

MINDFULNESS ON THE GO:
Simple Meditation Practice You Can Do Anywhere
by Jan Chozen Bays

THE POCKET CHÖGYAM TRUNGPA
Compiled and edited by Carolyn Rose Gimian

THE POCKET DALAI LAMA
Edited by Mary Craig

THE POCKET EMILY DICKINSON
Edited by Brenda Hillman

THE POCKET HAIKU
Compiled and translated by Sam Hamill

THE POCKET KEN WILBER
Edited by Colin Bigelow

THE POCKET PEMA CHÖDRÖN
Edited by Eden Steinberg

THE POCKET RUMI
Edited by Kabir Helminski

THE POCKET SAMURAI
Translated and edited by William Scott Wilson

THE POCKET THICH NHAT HANH
Compiled and edited by Melvin McLeod

THE POCKET THOMAS MERTON
Edited by Robert Inchausti

THE POCKET TIBETAN BUDDHISM READER
Edited by Reginald A. Ray

THE POCKET ZEN READER
Edited by Thomas Cleary

PRACTICING PEACE
by Pema Chödrön

SHAMBHALA: The Sacred Path of the Warrior
by Chögyam Trungpa

TAO TEH CHING by Lao Tzu
Translated by John C. H. Wu

TEACHINGS OF THE BUDDHA
Edited by Jack Kornfield